Power and Change

CONTRIBUTIONS TO NAVAL HISTORY... NO. 2

Power and Change

The Administrative History of the Office of the Chief of Naval Operations 1946-1986

Thomas C. Hone

Naval Historical Center
Department of the Navy
Washington, D.C. 1989

Library of Congress Cataloging-in-Publication Data

Hone, Thomas.
  Power and change

  (Contributions to naval history ; no. 2)
  Includes bibliographical references.
1. United States. Office of the Chief of Naval Operations—
History. I. Title. II. Series.
VA58.H58 1989   359.3′3042′0973   89-13266
ISBN 0-945274-02-5

For sale by the Superintendent of Documents, U.S. Government Printing Office
Washington, D.C. 20402

Contributions to Naval History Series

The Author

Thomas C. Hone received his Ph.D. in Political Science from the University of Wisconsin in 1973. He served as a faculty member at the Naval War College in Newport, Rhode Island, in 1986. While writing this study, Dr. Hone was an associate with Booz, Allen & Hamilton Inc. In 1988 he joined the Policy and Organizational Management Department of the Defense Systems Management College at Fort Belvoir, Virginia. Dr. Hone has contributed a chapter to *Air Leadership* (Washington: Office of Air Force History, 1986) and has published articles in a number of professional journals, including *Defense Analysis, Naval War College Review, Armed Forces and Society, The Journal of Strategic Studies, The Journal of Military History* (formerly *Military Affairs*), and the U.S. Naval Institute *Proceedings*.

Foreword

Power and Change is a study of the organizational development of the
Office of the Chief of Naval Operations (OPNAV) from the end of the
Second World War until the final years of the Reagan administration.
The story is set against the backdrop of the momentous and often
perplexing political, technological, and military developments of the
postwar decades and of a rapidly evolving and changing U.S. national
security organization.

In the four decades following the Second World War, the Office of the
Chief of Naval Operations underwent reorganization about every two
and a half years. There were eighteen Secretaries of the Navy and
fourteen Chiefs of Naval Operations. At the same time the organization
itself expanded and became more complex despite the efforts of the
Secretary of Defense and Congress to limit its size. Such rapid and far-
reaching changes would obviously tax the memory and the
understanding of even the most perceptive student of organizational
development. For this reason, we are pleased to offer this introduction to
the history of the Office of the Chief of Naval Operations to personnel
joining the organization. We are also confident that more experienced
members of the OPNAV and Secretariat staffs will find much of interest
here.

The Naval Historical Center was fortunate in securing the services of
Dr. Thomas C. Hone to prepare this study. Dr. Hone, a widely recognized
expert in naval history, combines extensive practical experience as a
management analyst with the historian's methodological training and
thorough familiarity with primary sources. Only the rare combination of
such skills could have produced this work.

With this study, the Naval Historical Center continues its series of
monographs in the recent history of the U.S. Navy begun by Michael A.
Palmer with *Origins of the Maritime Strategy*. Forthcoming works in the
series will deal with such topics as the design and construction of U.S.
submarines and the Navy and national security policy in the first
postwar decade. The views expressed herein are those of Dr. Hone, and
not those of the Department of the Navy or any other agency of the U.S.
Government.

Ronald H. Spector
Director of Naval History

Preface

This study chronicles and analyzes the changes in the organization and influence of the Office of the Chief of Naval Operations (OPNAV) from the end of the Second World War through most of John F. Lehman's tenure as Secretary of the Navy. The study is not exhaustive. Instead, it is an introduction to the evolution and workings of a complex organization that has struggled with major organizational, political, and technological challenges for more than two generations.

The story of OPNAV since 1945 touches on the three major military developments that have profoundly altered the executive branch of the U. S. Government in the four decades since the defeat of Imperial Japan and fascist Germany: (1) the creation of large standing military forces and the deployment of such forces on the periphery of the Soviet Union, (2) the development of institutions to control such forces and plan for their use, and (3) the establishment of a greatly expanded relationship between military organizations and private enterprises. The postwar history of OPNAV cannot be separated from these larger developments.

The changes in OPNAV in the last forty years are also related to individuals—both civilian and military—and their ideas about how naval forces should be organized, commanded, supported, and employed. What has happened to OPNAV—what the organization has become—cannot be understood without first comprehending the effects of individuals and their ideas on the structure and the processes that together make up the Navy Department. While the Navy and OPNAV have been strongly influenced by factors such as changes in military technology, the Navy by 1987 was very much a product of the actions of senior Navy officers and senior officials in the Navy Department and in the Defense Department.

It is often easier to discern the impact of larger factors, such as technology or financing, on organizations than it is to perceive the often subtle effects of individuals and small groups working through administrative routines. Their actual effects are often obscured by the organization's method of record keeping. In the Navy, for example, an initial on a headquarters memo is sometimes the only clue that an officer has witnessed and perhaps participated in the development of a policy. Indeed, official records may actually mislead a researcher, and the "truth" may be difficult to uncover even with the help of memoirs and oral histories. Nevertheless, OPNAV's postwar history is dominated by the actions and ideas of key individuals, especially James V. Forrestal,

Secretary of the Navy (from 1944 until his appointment as the first Secretary of Defense in 1947); Admiral Arleigh A. Burke, Chief of Naval Operations (1955-1961); Robert S. McNamara, Secretary of Defense (1961-1968); Admiral Elmo R. Zumwalt, Jr., Chief of Naval Operations (1970-1974); and John F. Lehman, Jr., Secretary of the Navy (1981-1987). More than any others, these men left their marks on OPNAV in the postwar period.

Together, individuals and events shaped the Office of the Chief of Naval Operations, and the study that follows will move back and forth from larger issues, such as debates over defense reorganization, to specific Navy concerns, such as the relationship between OPNAV and the Navy systems commands (former bureaus) charged with producing the weapons and equipment necessary for effective fleet operations. This history is not intended to cover in detail every significant event in the organizational life of OPNAV since the Second World War. Nor does it discuss the relationship between the Chief of Naval Operations and the Commandant of the Marine Corps. But the study will explain how OPNAV has changed and why. For details of changes in the Defense Department or in naval technology, readers are encouraged to consult other sources.

When first confronted with OPNAV's complex structure, the researcher must ask how it got to be that way. The office is not like other complex businesses or military commands in the United States. At times it functions more like a representative political organization than a military staff. Created to support the Chief of Naval Operations, OPNAV has often thwarted the efforts of the CNOs to shape naval forces and operations. It is fair to say that in the last twenty-five years CNOs have faced a major problem: preserving their influence against attempts by their own staffs and outsiders to dilute it. Hence, the recent history of OPNAV is one characterized by both bureaucratic infighting and honest efforts by officers, who disagree about the nature of war at sea, to shape the force structure and fighting doctrines of the Navy.

Coincident with this conflict is the struggle by the Office of the Secretary of Defense (OSD) to impose its authority on the separate services. In both cases—within the Navy and between the Navy and the Secretary of Defense—conflicts over policy and power are waged within the boundaries set by shared beliefs among most of the participants. The first and most important belief is the need for civilian control of U.S. military forces. Another shared view is the need for adequate operational and mobilization planning before war or conflict begins, so that the United States is not faced with the problems that hindered U.S. military mobilization in the months just before the Second World War. Still another common belief—stronger now than it was in 1946—is that the benefits of preserving the three major services (and the Marine Corps) outweigh the economic and organizational costs of interservice competition.

Within the Navy, the acceptance of separate services finds its counterpart in the acceptance of different combat specialties. Thus the day of the truly general line officer is gone. Officers and enlisted personnel must specialize earlier in their careers than they once did if the Navy is to be effective in combat. However, such specialization has an undesirable side effect: it promotes competition among the combat branches (submarine, surface, and air warfare) for limited fiscal and human resources. Each branch knows what it can do to win campaigns and wars, and each is confident that its contribution to victory deserves the stronger fiscal support from OPNAV. As a result, the Navy tends to fragment, making OPNAV an arena for intraservice conflict. Resolving this conflict in a way that will give the Navy the forces and manpower it needs has become the primary task of the CNO.

At first glance, the Office of the Chief of Naval Operations is a puzzling organization. The question, Who's in charge here? comes quickly to mind, as does the related query, How does it really work? This study will attempt to answer both questions and will also try to prove what Booz, Allen & Hamilton Inc. and the Director of Naval History believe—that the postwar organization of OPNAV cannot be understood without considering its rich and controversial history, especially its relations with both the Office of the Secretary of Defense and the Navy's material bureaus (later systems commands).

The study attempts to proceed chronologically, but many important events intertwine, making it difficult to divide the history into neat segments. The modern evolution of OPNAV is wedded to the development of the Office of the Secretary of Defense and to changes in military technology and U.S. strategy; each of these stories has its own timeline. Overlapping themes and interwoven chronologies bedevil the historian as they did the Chiefs of Naval Operations. The historian has the easier task: pulling together the threads of OPNAV policy and administration as the staff of the Chief of Naval Operations interacted with its superior (Office of the Secretary of Defense), its equals (Army and Air Force staffs), and its nominal—but often not actual—subordinates (Navy bureaus, or systems commands). Successive Chiefs of Naval Operations had to do the same thing in real time, without the benefit of hindsight and memoirs. Not surprisingly, CNOs have found the position extremely demanding.

Yet there are patterns. Since the Second World War, the service headquarters staffs have steadily lost influence to the unified and specified operational command staffs, to the Office of the Secretary of

Defense, and to the Joint Staff of the Joint Chiefs of Staff (JCS). Uniformed military leaders, Congress, and several Presidents are responsible for this shift in influence. Their legislation and official instructions marked the road for the headquarters' staffs. It is this well-publicized route, affecting all three services, that this study will generally follow.

The process by which defense (as against service) management changed over time will be linked to changes in the way the Navy has been run by considering the major studies initiated by the Navy since the Second World War. Examples of these studies are those conducted by the Gates Committee (1954), the Libby Board (1956), the Franke Board (1959), the Dillon Board (1962), and the Benson Task Force (1966), as well as later studies commissioned by the Chiefs of Naval Operations in the 1960s and 1970s. Similarly, changes in Navy force structure will be traced with reference to major changes in U.S. strategy. The study will move back and forth from internal Navy issues to external developments that drove, or were driven by, those Navy issues.

The purpose of the study is to show how and why OPNAV's structure and patterns of operation changed in the forty years after the Second World War. The work is not a critique, although it is quite analytical. The analysis is necessary to tie together and give meaning to OPNAV's history. OPNAV is not just complex. It is also confusing—even frustrating—to those who have to work within it and deal with it. Hence, a study of this type must create order where disorder seems to rule. It must apply concepts to human action to clarify the reasons for that action.

The Office of the Chief of Naval Operations is not the way it is by accident. To understand why and how OPNAV has become the organization it is, the analyst and historian must present its modern history in the context of what organizations are supposed to do. In plain terms, the Office of the Chief of Naval Operations must be understood as an organization assigned certain crucial tasks. How it carried out those tasks and how the nature of the tasks themselves changed over time are central topics of this study.

Acknowledgments

This study could not have been conducted without the help of four groups of people. The first group includes the archivists of the Navy's Operational Archives, located in the Washington Navy Yard, and Mr. Charles A. Meyers of the Organization and OPNAV Resources Management Division (OP-09B2) in the Pentagon. Of the former, Mr. Bernard F. Cavalcante was particularly helpful. He suggested the records of the Deputy Chief of Naval Operations for Plans, Policy, and Operations (OP-06), which proved to be an invaluable resource. The study could not have been completed in the six months allowed without the aid of Mr. Cavalcante and his staff.

The second group consists of the Director of Naval History, Dr. Ronald H. Spector; officials of Booz, Allen & Hamilton Inc., especially Rear Admiral Kleber S. Masterson, Jr., USN (Ret.) and Captain George Thibault, USN (Ret.); and Professor Vincent Davis, Director of the Patterson School of Diplomacy and International Commerce at the University of Kentucky. All four strongly supported the study, respecting the author's judgement on sources and issues and answering his many questions. The third group consists of people who provided material, ideas, expertise, or critical readings of an initial draft of this study. Drs. Michael A. Palmer and Jeffrey G. Barlow, historians on the staff of the Naval Historical Center's Contemporary History Branch, freely shared ideas and insights based on their own research. Mr. Robert Downey of the Center for Naval Analyses drew on his years of experience in Navy Department budgeting to explain the importance of the Planning, Programming, and Budgeting System (PPBS). Captains Donald Stoufer, USN (Ret.), now with Booz, Allen & Hamilton, and John Fedor, USN (Ret.), agreed to interviews; both made very helpful comments. Captain Charles Allen, USN (Ret.), and Dr. Irving Blickstein of OP-090 commented on preliminary study outlines. Vice Admiral Kleber S. Masterson, USN (Ret.), former head of the Bureau of Naval Weapons, read a draft of the study, as did Captains Jake W. Stewart, Jr., USN (Ret.); Peter M. Swartz, USN; and John L. Byron, USN. Captains Stewart, Swartz, and Byron were especially supportive. All three dropped whatever they were doing and rescued the author from the complicated maze of OPNAV puzzles. Captain Byron of the National Defense University offered strong support all along. So, too, did Dr. Dean C. Allard, Senior Historian at the Naval Historical Center, whose knowledge of the modern Navy is immense.

The fourth group consists of the members of a final manuscript review panel: Mr. Robert Murray, Director of the National Security Program of the John F. Kennedy School of Government, Harvard University; Dr. Spector, Dr. William R. Braisted, Dr. Edward J. Marolda, Dr. Allard, and Dr. Barlow of the Naval Historical Center; Captain Byron; and Dr. Blickstein. All made helpful comments and suggestions.

Special recognition and thanks go to Ms. Sandra J. Doyle of the Contemporary History Branch for editing the manuscript and preparing the index and to the *Naval Aviation News* staff, especially Mr. Charles C. Cooney for layout and cover design and JO1 James G. Richeson for typesetting.

The Office of the Chief of Naval Operations is a large, complex organization with a long, complicated history. It would be presumptuous to believe that the most complex piece of that history could be wrapped up in less than two hundred pages after six months of research and writing. Hence, any errors of fact in the pages which follow are the author's alone, and are not to be blamed on Booz, Allen & Hamilton, on the Director of Naval History, or on any of those who provided assistance to the author. This history was produced by Booz, Allen & Hamilton for the Director of Naval History and the Principal Deputy Assistant to the Secretary of the Navy for Research, Engineering, and Systems. It does not represent the official views of the Department of Navy.

Contents

Illustrations

U.S. Navy, Air Force, and Army photographs are held by the Still Media Records Center, Department of Defense, Washington, D.C. 20374-1681. The Naval Historical Center holds copies of all other photographs.

Introduction

The Office of the Chief of Naval Operations (OPNAV) has lost statutory authority since 1946 because of a series of changes in the laws that regulate national security decision making. In 1945, for example, the Chief of Naval Operations (CNO) was also the Commander in Chief, U.S. Fleet (COMINCH). The distinction COMINCH/CNO was dropped after the Second World War, and the CNO was briefly senior operational and administrative commander. In 1946, however, the great administrative and command powers held by the Chief of Naval Operations began to decline when the military services agreed to establish peacetime unified commands in each major theater of operations. Between January and December 1947, the President created by executive order seven unified commands. These commands were the forerunners of today's CINCs such as CINCPAC (Commander in Chief, Pacific). Since 1946 the command authority of what are now called the unified and specified commands has grown, while that of the CNO has declined. Indeed, since 1958 the Chief of Naval Operations has wielded no statutory control of Navy forces. His influence over operations is now applied, if at all, through his participation in the Joint Chiefs of Staff (JCS).

Congress and several Presidents have also created a strong Department of Defense, beginning in 1949 with amendments to the National Security Act of 1947. The amendments reduced the status of the military services from executive departments to agencies subordinate to the Secretary of Defense. The process of centralizing authority in the Secretary of Defense and the Joint Chiefs of Staff continued in 1953, when an executive order directed the service chiefs to make their work on the JCS their first priority. That same year Congress gave the Secretary of Defense the authority to create "single manager" agencies such as the Defense Mapping Agency. President Dwight D. Eisenhower, a proponent of increased service cooperation, returned to Congress in 1958 with a proposal to diminish the command powers of the service chiefs, including the CNO. Congress turned that proposal into law.

The new powers of the Secretary of Defense were made clear in 1961, when Secretary of Defense Robert S. McNamara imposed the Planning, Programming, and Budgeting System (PPBS) on the services. This system replaced the Navy's own programming methods and further increased the authority of the Office of the Secretary of Defense (OSD). In 1986 Congress increased the authority of the Chairman of the JCS and the unified theater commanders. The 1986 reforms were intended to focus authority and responsibility on a senior military official, the Chairman of the JCS, but they also advanced the forty-year process of weakening the powers of the Chief of Naval Operations. With his command power gone and his administrative power limited by a strong Office of the Secretary of Defense, the CNO's influence was based less on what he could order people to do than on what he could persuade people, especially the Navy and Defense secretaries and other service chiefs, to believe.

CNOs faced another problem in the years after the Second World War: "governing" OPNAV, the entire Office of the Chief of Naval Operations. In 1939 the officers in OPNAV represented about two percent of all the officers in the Navy; in 1985, about four percent—not a drastic increase. However, the increase in absolute numbers is impressive and indicative of a major problem. In 1939 there were 129 officers in OPNAV. By 1985 that number had increased to nearly 1,500. The purpose of OPNAV is to assist the CNO, but as the office grew, it became in some ways an obstacle to CNOs, if only because of its size. There is a parallel between Presidents, who must use (and not be used by) White House offices, and CNOs, who must count on the support of the OPNAV offices that they govern.

A comparison between OPNAV's 1947 and 1986 organizations reveals the decline in the CNO's ability to control OPNAV. In 1947, OPNAV was organized functionally with Deputy Chiefs of Naval Operations (DCNOs) for personnel, administration, operations, logistics, and air. In effect, the functional deputies had Navy-wide perspectives and their responsibilities cut across the warfare, or platform, communities. The exception to the functional pattern was the deputy for air. All other deputy chiefs considered problems and needs that were common to the Navy's operating forces, whether they moved on, above, or below the sea. In 1986 the principal deputies were for program planning, naval warfare, research and development, personnel, submarine warfare, surface warfare, air warfare, plans and policies, and logistics. The deputies with responsibilities that crossed warfare boundaries, such as program planning, shared influence with deputies whose responsibilities focused within a warfare area such as submarine warfare.

By the mid-1980s the Office of the Chief of Naval Operations had become three rather distinct suboffices. The first directly served the CNO and was composed of program planning, naval warfare, and research and development. The second was composed of the deputy chiefs for submarine, surface, and air warfare, who sought to act with the CNO's authority on matters related to their specialties. The third was the plans and policy wing of OPNAV, which supported the CNO's role as a member of the Joint Chiefs of Staff. The growth of OPNAV and the growing complexity of naval warfare made it difficult for any one office to coordinate all the missions and needs of the Navy. Yet the development of suboffices made it harder, not easier, for CNOs to affect the Navy. By the 1980s no CNO could assume that his own staff was a loyal and effective instrument that he could use to shape the Navy.

The CNO's primary problem today is that he must lead the Navy even though he cannot command it. That was also his problem before the Second World War. His task then was to prepare the Navy for war by drawing up strategic plans, setting guidelines for training and exercises, specifying the weapon and equipment needs of the fleet for the Navy's bureaus, and advising the President. The administrative burden on the CNO and OPNAV was alleviated then by the Navy's form of decentralized organization. The CNO and his staff set the guidelines and policies for the fleet, shore stations, and bureaus, but actual command of these organizations was delegated to others. After 1966, however, that pattern of administration was abandoned when OPNAV assumed more control over the bureaus. The negative consequence of the change, unfortunately, was an increase in the administrative burden on the CNO and on OPNAV.

As the CNO's real authority has declined, his workload has increased. Moreover, this burden has been administrative and bureaucratic, not operational. As a result, CNOs have become frustrated by their apparent inability to get things done. However, the office retains great potential. The CNO can have great influence over Navy spending, manpower assessments and assignments, training, naval strategy, and the Navy's programs of development and acquisition. As a member of the Joint Chiefs of Staff, the CNO can also influence, though not command, military operations, and he has access to major political figures such as the Secretary of Defense and the President.

The Chief of Naval Operations is in some ways like the modern President: much of his real power springs from convincing subordinates and then audiences outside the department that they ought to share his goals and concerns. To be effective, a CNO must work through several complex organizations—including OPNAV, the Navy systems commands, and Congress—by capturing the loyalty and imagination of their members.

NOTE: The numbering system for the Office of the Chief of Naval Operations can be confusing to those not familiar with the organization. The DCNOs are given two-digit codes beginning with zero, OP-03, for example. Their immediate subordinates are also given two-digit codes, with the first digit indicating the DCNO office, as in OP-35. The next level down is given a three-digit code, such as OP-354. The level below that has three digits plus a letter, such as OP-354C.

Administration versus Command

For most of the twentieth century, the Navy has faced serious organizational issues within itself and in Congress. In his careful study, *The Admirals Lobby*, published in 1967, Vincent Davis argued that the cause was a unique characteristic of the Navy's culture—its commitment to what Davis called "pluralistic decentralization."[1] As Davis noted, this commitment to decentralized authority and decision making had mixed consequences. Naval officers, traditionally independent, were also taught to take initiative and exercise authority. This in turn created a corps of officers who instinctively resisted central control. At its best, the tradition encouraged responsibility and innovation; at its worst, it justified bureaucratic infighting.

Before the Second World War, the Navy's tradition of independent command and decentralized authority was reflected in its structure. The "old" Navy was a set of fiefdoms—the bureaus ashore and the commander in chief at sea with the fleet. The Navy ashore was dominated internally by its bureaus, especially Ordnance, Navigation, and Aeronautics headed by line officers. These offices had direct links with Congress. Before 1921 the bureaus even had separate appropriations accounts approved by Congress. There was no single chief military administrator until 1915 when Congress authorized the creation of the Chief of Naval Operations. Even then the bureau chiefs and fleet commanders continued to be highly influential—sometimes dominant—through and after the First World War until the positions of CNO and Commander in Chief, U.S. Fleet, were combined in 1942.

The desire to avoid (rather than confront) centralized authority kept the Office of the Chief of Naval Operations small and allowed fleet commanders and bureau chiefs to avoid strong supervision. But decentralization almost cost the Navy its aviation arm when Army airmen aggressively pressed Congress for a separate air service after the First World War.[2] The Navy again lost the political initiative to the Army after the Second World War, when many War Department leaders, including the civilian secretary, argued in favor of complete service unification. In each case—the struggle for aviation after the First World War and the fight over unification after the Second World War—certain senior officers, who were unafraid of political activity and therefore capable of bureaucratic maneuvering, fiercely protected the Navy's interest.[3]

Although line officers were trained in staff work, and many spent time in administrative posts in Navy bureaus such as Ordnance and Aeronautics, many would have agreed with one destroyerman-turned-aviator, who noted in his memoirs, "'Politics' had never touched me."[4] However, after both world wars, the Navy found itself in need of officers whom "politics" had touched. It was not enough for the Navy to be advanced in technology and tactics. The Navy needed shrewd leaders who could win political support for new programs and shield the service from partisan attacks. After the First World War naval aviation interests were represented in Washington by just such a leader, Rear Admiral William A. Moffett, the first chief of the Bureau of Aeronautics (BUAER).[5] After the Second World War the challenges to the Navy were even greater. New bureaucratic infighters like Captain (later Vice Admiral) Hyman G. Rickover, "father" of the nuclear-powered Navy, generated other problems as their political successes threatened both the power and prestige of postwar CNOs while simultaneously adding to the Navy's apparent strength.[6]

In June 1933 Representative Carl Vinson (D-Georgia), Chairman of the House Naval Affairs Committee, submitted a bill to reorganize OPNAV. Vinson wanted to create, under the CNO, an Office of Naval Material to coordinate the activities of the major support bureaus of Construction and Repair, Steam Engineering, Ordnance, and Aeronautics. He also favored creating a set of offices subordinate to the Secretary of the Navy (instead of to the CNO) that would coordinate Navy strategic planning with the Army.[7] The Navy's response, developed through hearings before the General Board, a panel of admirals who advised the Secretary of the Navy, opposed strengthening OPNAV for several reasons. First, a strong Chief of Naval Operations might threaten civilian control. Second, senior Navy officers did not want to enlarge the secretary's office and give it direct supervision of material procurement. That move would put the bureaus under day-to-day civilian management instead of ultimate civilian authority. *Responsibility* to the secretary was acceptable; *control* by the secretary was not. Third, they objected to the complexity of the proposed reorganization. If change were required, then all that was needed was an increase in the powers of the CNO so that he could direct the bureaus. But since the bureaus worked well together already, that drastic step, which the bureaus opposed, was not necessary.[8] These were the basic arguments that senior Navy officers would present successfully for the next thirty years when confronted by congressional or presidential pressures to restructure the Navy or OPNAV.

On 18 December 1941 Congress approved the First War Powers Act (Public Law 354, 77th Congress), specifying President Franklin D.

Roosevelt's authority as Commander in Chief. That same day Roosevelt issued Executive Order 8984, defining the duties of the Chief of Naval Operations and the Commander in Chief, U.S. Fleet. The CNO was responsible for training, planning, intelligence collection, and preparing warships for operations. The Commander in Chief, U.S. Fleet, was charged with organizing the fleet, executing war plans, and informing the CNO of fleet needs.

In the spring of 1942, however, Admiral Ernest J. King (COMINCH) and Admiral Harold K. Stark (CNO) persuaded President Roosevelt to consolidate the two positions. On 12 March 1942 the President signed Executive Order 9096, which stated that the new COMINCH/CNO was "the principal naval advisor to the President on the conduct of the War, and the principal naval advisor and executive to the Secretary of the Navy on the conduct of the activities of the Naval Establishment." The order also established a chief of staff to the Commander in Chief, U.S. Fleet, and a Vice Chief of Naval Operations (VCNO) to assist the CNO. The following day Roosevelt nominated King for the CNO position. As COMINCH/CNO, King received the authority to direct the actions "of the bureaus and offices of the Navy Department except such offices (other than bureaus) as the Secretary of the Navy may specifically exempt." With this order, the Chief of Naval Operations received what some senior officers had always wanted: control of both the fleet and the material bureaus. These officers, among them King, had not expressed their aspirations to Vinson before the war because they did not want members of Congress to interpret their position as a challenge to civilian control of the Navy.

Despite the consolidation of military authority in the office of the CNO, James V. Forrestal, appointed Under Secretary of the Navy in August 1940, believed some added civilian direction of the material bureaus was also necessary. On taking office, he was appalled by the sorry state of the Navy's material procurement administration. Having served in OPNAV during the First World War, he had witnessed the managed growth of naval aviation from a token force to a major organization with 7,000 officers, 33,000 enlisted personnel, and over 2,100 aircraft.[9] He could not see in 1940 the same ability in the uniformed Navy to mobilize the resources of American industry, and he criticized the Bureau of Supplies and Accounts for failing to adapt effectively to mobilization.

With the support of Secretary of the Navy Frank Knox, Forrestal created the Office of Procurement and Material to impose civilian direction on the procurement process managed by the Navy's bureaus (e.g.,Ordnance, Aeronautics, and Supplies and Accounts).[10] In effect, Forrestal became the Navy's chief procurement officer and made the new office a focal point for relations between the Navy and civilian industry, while King directed Navy planning and set the requirements for Navy construction and procurement. The relationship between the CNO and the under secretary was neither cordial nor close. King wanted to direct the Navy's war effort and to advise the President on the overall course of the campaign against the Axis powers. Forrestal disputed King's direction of Navy procurement and the admiral's control of the Navy's bureaus. In 1943, while Forrestal was still under secretary, King proposed creating five deputy chiefs of naval operations and giving them the authority to act for the CNO in the areas of their responsibility. Forrestal opposed the move on the grounds that it would dilute the authority of the Secretary of the Navy by creating centers of responsibility removed from direct contact with the secretary's office. The under secretary prevailed.[11]

In April 1944 Secretary Knox died suddenly, and Forrestal was sworn in as Navy secretary the following month. Drawing on the secretary's statutory powers, Forrestal implemented the recommendations of a

NH 62563

Fleet Admiral Chester W. Nimitz (*left*) with Secretary of the Navy James Forrestal on Guam, 1945.

management study of the Secretariat undertaken by the presidents of General Motors and United States Steel. He first created the post of fiscal director (later comptroller) in the Office of the Secretary of the Navy. He then put together the Top Policy Group, composed of the Navy's senior military and civilian officials in Washington, to serve as a "board of directors." At the group's first meeting he announced the creation of an organizational review, study, and planning unit headed by the Navy's inspector general, but actually led by Commander Richard M. Paget, USNR, a successful management consultant from the firm of Booz, Allen & Hamilton.[12] Forrestal directed the new Organization Planning and Procedure Unit to determine how the Navy should be organized in the postwar period.

Within four days of Japan's surrender, Forrestal created another special board to consider the Navy's postwar organization. It was headed by Under Secretary of the Navy Artemus L. Gates, a naval aviator in the First World War and Assistant Secretary of the Navy for Air in the Second World War. The other members of the Gates Committee were members of Forrestal's Top Policy Group. On 7 November 1945 the board produced a report entitled "Recommendations Concerning the Executive Administration of the Naval Establishment." On 12 January 1946 Forrestal accepted the report's recommendations, later promulgated in Navy General Order Number 230. In it, OPNAV was given responsibility for producing what are now called operational requirements—the standards that new weapons and equipment must meet. The Office of the Secretary of the Navy was given the authority to manage actual procurement—to deal directly with civilian suppliers. These two activities, referred to respectively as "consumer" and "producer" logistics, remained separate for another twenty years.[13]

Forrestal also persuaded President Harry S. Truman to issue a new statement of the CNO's authority (Executive Order 9635 of 29 September 1945), which superseded Executive Orders 8984 of 1941 and 9096 of 1942. Admiral King was not pleased with the new executive order, however, because it made the CNO "principal advisor to the President *and* to the Secretary of the Navy"; charged him, "*under* the direction of the Secretary of the Navy, with the preparation, readiness and logistic support of the operating forces"; divided the supervisory authority over the Navy's material bureaus between the secretary and the CNO; and created a new office to coordinate scientific research that would report to the secretary. Truman's executive order authorized the appointments of Deputy Chiefs of Naval Operations, but left the decision of how many to the Secretary of the Navy. The new mandate gave the CNO authority over the Navy's bureaus, but made it clear that this authority was neither separate from nor superior to the authority of the Navy secretary. Forrestal had won his organizational victory over King, and when Fleet Admiral Chester W. Nimitz succeeded King as CNO, the secretary extracted from Nimitz an agreement that the new deputy chiefs would be "mutually agreeable" to both officials.[14]

The official powers of the CNO were later identified in General Order Number 5 of 10 February 1947: (a) "command of the Operating Forces," (b) "principal naval advisor to the President and the Secretary," (c) "promulgation to the bureaus . . . of such directives as he deems necessary with respect to matters of operations," (d) "planning and forecasting the needs of the Operating Forces," (e) "issuing statements of these requirements . . . to the bureaus," (f) "reviewing and evaluating the progress of the bureaus," and (g) assisting the Secretary of the Navy "in the formulation of policies and procedures governing the administration of the Naval Establishment." Just over a year later, the 80th Congress enacted these orders in Public Law 432, which stated that the duty of the CNO was "to command the operating forces and be responsible to the Secretary of the Navy for their use, including, but not limited to, their training, readiness, and preparation for war, and plans

80-G-482803

The Navy Department Building on 18th and Constitution Avenue in Washington served as headquarters for the Secretary of the Navy and the Chief of Naval Operations until 1948 when the offices moved to the Pentagon.

Secretary of the Navy James
Forrestal in his office.
80-G-K-6842

therefor." Under the direction of the Navy secretary, the CNO was given
the authority to "determine the personnel and material requirements of
the operating forces," and to "coordinate and direct the efforts of the
bureaus and offices of the Navy Department as may be necessary to
effectuate availability and distribution of the personnel and material
required where and when they are needed." The law also allowed the
CNO to have six deputy chiefs, each with the authority to issue orders
"considered as emanating from the Chief of Naval Operations."

King had not liked Forrestal's proposals because they simultaneously
increased the powers of the CNO and the Navy secretary. The admiral's
concern, which he had first voiced soon after becoming COMINCH in
December 1941, was that the leadership of the Navy would be
divided. Forrestal's concern, by comparison, was that increasing the
powers of the CNO without concurrently bolstering the authority of the
Navy secretary would weaken civilian control of the Navy. The postwar
Executive Order 9635, General Order Number 5, and Public Law 432 were
written to satisfy both King and Forrestal by increasing the powers of the
CNO while keeping him clearly subordinate to the Navy's civilian
leadership.

Forrestal's concerns for the powers of the Navy secretary stemmed not
only from his commitment to civilian control. In April 1944, just before
the death of Secretary Knox, the Congressional Select Committee on
Post-War Military Policy, chaired by Representative Clifton A. Woodrum
(D-Virginia.), heard the testimony of Army and Navy civilian and

military leaders to consider whether wartime command experience suggested any postwar changes to the organization or command of the military services. The hearings made it clear to Forrestal that the Army planned to push hard for unification of the armed services even before the war was over. Forrestal also perceived that Navy planning for the postwar period was based on the assumption that the service could resume its prewar role independent from the Army. Forrestal was convinced that the days of independent service planning were over. He knew that the Navy would find defending its postwar operations difficult unless it showed that naval power could apply military pressure against the increasingly hostile Soviet Union. But uniformed planners "could not foresee a precise task for the postwar Navy."[15]

Forrestal believed that the Navy needed civilian leadership to confront the unification issue and to stake out a role in postwar strategic planning. To Forrestal the unification debate was essentially political. Unlike Admiral King, he feared that the very existence of the Navy as a separate force might be at stake. Once confirmed as Secretary of the Navy, Forrestal responded to the threat of unification by cultivating public opinion in favor of a strong, independent Navy. At the same time Forrestal began talking publicly about the Soviet Union as the likely enemy in the next war. He exhorted Navy officers to think about means of using naval forces to attack the Soviet Union and to face problems outside the traditional Pacific arena. He also changed the character of Navy leadership by accelerating the process whereby naval aviators reached top command positions.[16]

As early as summer 1945, Secretary Forrestal was working to develop a unified strategy for dealing with what he thought were the major problems facing the Navy and for preparing the Navy organizationally for the postwar world. Indeed, his success in the first task helped him immeasurably in the second. Navy officers who might have opposed his claims to civilian control had to admit that the secretary was leading an effective defense against the advocates of service unification.

During the struggle with the Army over service unification, Forrestal helped that group of officers which he thought might likely help him in return. On 4 December 1945 he announced that half of the important positions below the CNO level in OPNAV would go to aviators and that, for the first time, aviators would be as eligible for fleet commands as other line officers.[17] At Forrestal's request, President Truman asked Congress to lower the statutory retirement age for officers and to increase the authorized peacetime strength of the Navy while making room for a higher proportion of officers.[18] Congress did both, with the result that the proportion of aviators among all Navy officers and within the ranks of flag officers increased markedly, despite the effects of demobilization.[19]

As Davis noted, however, "the forthcoming dominance of aviation forces in the postwar Navy was not decided in response to a new strategic concept or to an analysis of the international political situation but rather in response to an institutional threat to the Navy which originated within the domestic political arena."[20] Finally, in October 1945, Forrestal—on the advice of aviator Vice Admiral Arthur W. Radford—established what became known as the Secretary's Committee on Research on Reorganization (SCOROR). This committee was Forrestal's counsel in the legislative struggle over service unification.[21]

In his study of Navy postwar planning, Davis observed that Navy planners avoided "contact with all other parts of the government in an effort to conduct the planning in as much privacy—indeed, secrecy—as possible."[22] Forrestal well understood that such an approach was a political mistake and would be futile in the postwar strategic setting. As the war ended, he planned to drag the Navy away from its institutional isolation and independent action toward more involvement with the other services and the influential public. Yet to move the Navy, he had to rein in the CNO, increase the prestige and influence of the office of the secretary, open spots in the Navy's hierarchy for naval aviators, and fight the Navy's prejudice against allowing the secretary to become actively involved in what had been traditionally considered strictly military matters, such as strategic planning. Forrestal was committed to heading the Navy away from its institutional culture of the prewar years.

80-G-396228

Postwar testing of the atomic bomb at Bikini Atoll. "Baker Day," 25 July 1946, of Operation Crossroads.

2

Postwar Challenges

Postwar conflicts among the services—especially between the newly created Air Force and the Navy—over organization and strategy frustrated or embittered almost every senior civilian and military official then serving in the defense of the United States. In addition to setting the Navy and Air Force on a collision course, the new military technology developed during the Second World War posed particularly severe tactical and budgetary problems for the Navy. The prospect that the Soviet Navy would build on captured German technology to produce large numbers of submarines with high submerged speed and underwater endurance, for example, promised to make the Navy's antisubmarine equipment, ships, and tactics obsolete within five years. The development of nuclear weapons also threatened the Navy's strategic role. In August 1945 no operational Navy carrier attack plane could loft an atomic bomb. Only the Army Air Forces' B-29s could carry the bulky 5-ton weapons, and then only after special modifications, which left the aircraft unable to carry conventional bombs, were made. If naval aircraft could not carry nuclear weapons, then what role did the Navy's carriers have in a future global war? Indeed, if future conflict with the Soviet Union were to be exclusively nuclear, then what was the purpose of the Navy? Showing that the Navy had a real strategic mission in an age of nuclear weapons was hard enough. It was an even more difficult task in the immediate postwar years, when conventional forces were rapidly demobilized because funding for them was considered inflationary.[1]

The Army Air Forces espoused the new nuclear technology, but its leaders understood the need for new equipment and a special force to carry atomic weapons.[2] As strategic analyst Norman Friedman noted, nuclear weapons "threatened to make existing forms of warfare obsolete," so the need to develop atomic weapons and machines to carry them in a climate hostile to maintaining expensive and large military organizations immediately caused a fiscal squeeze.[3] The lack of money, moreover, forced both the Air Force and the Navy into a zero-sum game, the details of which are documented elsewhere.[4] But it is important to note the degree to which the conflict between the Navy and the Army, and after 1947 between the Navy and the Air Force, over the nature of war in the nuclear age affected the attitudes of Navy officers toward service unification and interservice cooperation. By 1948 senior Navy officers interpreted calls for unification as a pretense for dismembering the Naval Establishment—by transferring naval aviation units to the Air Force and the Marines to the Army.

Secretary of the Navy Forrestal sensed some of the approaching problems even before Japan surrendered. In September 1945 he accepted a report covering the arguments for and against service unification, prepared by Ferdinand Eberstadt, an old friend and colleague from business and government service. Impressed with Eberstadt's analysis, Forrestal forwarded it to Senator David Walsh, Chairman of the Naval Affairs Committee. Walsh had it printed under the title "Unification of the War and Navy Departments and Postwar Organization for National Security."[5] Eberstadt's analysis was so persuasive that the National Security Act of 1947 (Public Law 253) basically followed its recommendations. To match the publicity given "air power," Forrestal also tried unsuccessfully to persuade Congress to give the Navy's Office of Public Relations bureau status. He was committed, nonetheless, to publicizing the Navy's case and improving the Navy's reputation among the public, especially in preparation for the debates over unification and service roles and missions.[6]

The Joint Congressional Committee investigation of the Japanese attack on Pearl Harbor also spurred the calls for military reorganization. The hearings, which began in Washington on 15 November 1945 and continued until mid-July 1946, revealed that the officers in command in Hawaii in 1941 were not fully aware of the nature of U.S.-Japanese relations. Those officers suggested that the defeat at Pearl Harbor might not have happened if they had been closer to the President in the chain of command. Their testimony gave the advocates of establishing peacetime theater and specified commands more support. Atomic weapons made the need for such commands even more imperative. To avoid future Pearl Harbors, the committee recommended peacetime "unity of command;" that is, one overall military commander in each primary theater of operations.[7] In 1947, after a bitter dispute between the Army and Navy over the authority required by these commands, President Truman created seven unified commands.[8]

The Pearl Harbor investigation also gave the Army's air leaders more justification to make the Strategic Air Command (SAC), established in March 1946, the primary strategic striking arm of the United States. That September, when Secretary Forrestal announced that the Navy would maintain a large force permanently in the Mediterranean, the Army's Assistant Chief of Staff for Intelligence told General Carl Spaatz, Commander Army Air Forces, that the Navy's decision was just a ploy to gain political support for a large naval force.[9] The Navy reciprocated this mistrust by questioning the ability of Army, and later Air Force, bombers to reach the right targets with the right weapons in the early stages of a war with the Soviet Union.

The disputes about service unification and about service roles and missions were rooted in the uncertainties created by technological change. For example, early jet aircraft accelerated slowly, and the catapults on Navy carriers in service in 1945 were not strong enough to assist the early jets to launch speed. The situation worsened when planes carried nuclear weapons. Such aircraft needed special boost engines to lift off a carrier's deck. Indeed, one reason the Navy so strongly opposed service unification in 1946 was because it seemed that the Army Air Forces were correct in their claim that carrier aircraft had no future role in strategic warfare. As Vice Admiral Robert B. Carney, Deputy Chief of Naval Operations for Logistics (OP-04), phrased it in an "Eyes Only" memo for CNO Nimitz in November 1946: "The entire role of aviation, as understood in 1945, may be due for an enforced change as a result of (a) aircraft improvement, and (b) the difficulties in adjusting carrier characteristics to further aircraft improvement." Carney was blunt: "Current trends in the weight, size, speed, and characteristics of aircraft may have a serious adverse effect on the utility of existing carriers and even on the overall importance of carrier aviation in the future."[10] In short, the Navy did in fact have reasonable doubts about the future of carrier aviation. The Navy was not the only service with doubts about its future in nuclear warfare, however. Even the Strategic Air Command was not well prepared for the new technology of nuclear weapons.

Given the climate of fiscal stringency, neither the Navy nor the Air Force dared to admit the technological uncertainties facing them after the war. Any such admission would be ammunition for the other side in the "war" over unification and service roles and missions. This did not mean there were not any real issues dividing the services. The debates over how to use nuclear weapons against the Soviet Union if war broke out and the disputes over the value of conventional forces in a war fought with nuclear weapons were bitter.

The Navy's internal problems stemmed from the postwar structure put together by Admiral King and his deputies during the war. Before the war a smaller Office of the Chief of Naval Operations—in relative and absolute terms—focused on three activities: planning (including military intelligence), operations (including training, maintenance of the fleet, and technical advances), and setting standards in areas like communications. During the war Admiral King attempted to make OPNAV a functionally organized headquarters, with directorates for personnel, logistics, transportation, and material. King also decided that OPNAV needed another kind of directorate, one which was linked directly with the Bureau of Aeronautics.

BUAER was unique among the Navy's major bureaus because its chief had both support and personnel responsibilities. Rear Admiral Moffett demanded and got extensive authority for his organization on the grounds that aviation needed and deserved special protection in its fledgling years.[11] By 1941, BUAER specialists designed and supervised the procurement of aircraft and had a hand in specifying aircraft carrier designs. The Bureau of Aeronautics also supervised the training of pilots and other air personnel, and worked with the Bureau of Navigation (the Navy's personnel office) in determining career ladders for aviators. As COMINCH/CNO, King, who had served as BUAER chief before the Second World War, supported the continued existence of the bureau. However, in late 1942 King created the position of Deputy Chief of Naval Operations for Air (OP-05) and gave this new office responsibility for all aviation personnel and their training. The new deputy chief also determined the number of flag billets in aviation commands at sea and ashore.[12] King's action gave naval aviation new visibility and organizational prestige, but it also reduced the potential for independent action by the Bureau of Aeronautics.

King had apparently considered adding other DCNO positions for submarines and for surface combatants, but both Secretary Knox and his successor, Forrestal, consistently blocked his proposals for reorganizing OPNAV. Consequently, the Office of the Chief of Naval Operations emerged from the war with both functional and weapons directorates: deputy chiefs for Personnel (OP-01), Administration (OP-02), Operations (OP-03), Logistics (OP-04), Air (OP-05), and Special Weapons (OP-06), disestablished in 1946. In 1939 none of the five flag officers in OPNAV below the CNO and the assistant chief held rank greater than that of rear admiral (two-star). After the war, however, all the deputy chief positions were filled by vice admirals, and rear admirals served as their senior assistants. Flag officers also directed the OPNAV offices of naval intelligence and communications, and a full admiral served as Navy Inspector General (OP-08). This was a major change from OPNAV's prewar structure. (See Figure 1.)

In this postwar organization, functional deputies (e.g., Personnel) worked alongside deputies for weapons (e.g., Air). Functional deputies administered areas that stretched across what are now referred to as the major warfare, or platform, communities—the aviators, submariners, and surface ship officers. The weapons deputies, especially the DCNO for Air, gave their communities a form of vested representation in the Navy's top policy-making institution. The tension that developed between the functional and the platform community deputies became a major issue within OPNAV over the next twenty-five years.

The new shape of OPNAV also demonstrated that it would not lose the powers that it had been given during the war. Before the Second World

OFFICE OF THE CHIEF OF NAVAL OPERATIONS, 1947

Figure 1

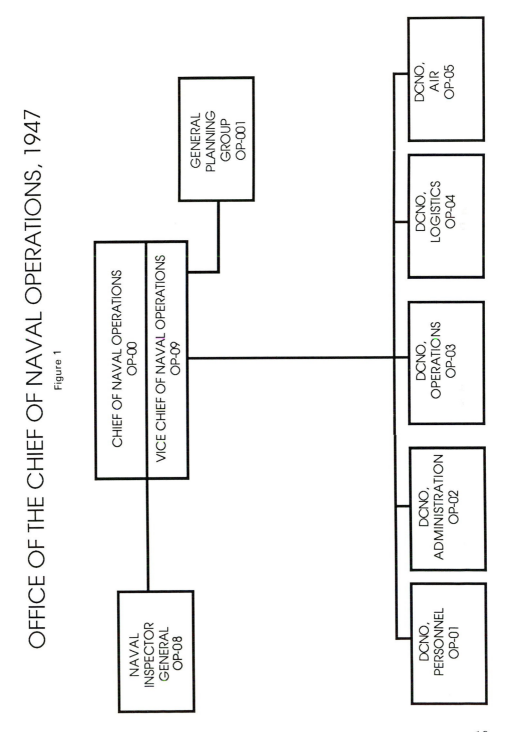

War, the uniformed Navy was divided into three organizations: the fleet, OPNAV, and the bureaus. The latter reported to the Secretary of the Navy and ultimately to Congress, thereby retaining potential independence from OPNAV. During the war, Admiral King moved to reduce the independence of the bureaus. Prewar ship designs, for example, were prepared within the Bureau of Ships (BUSHIPS) and then reviewed by the General Board, which forwarded the designs it approved to the Secretary of the Navy. The General Board was a panel of senior flag officers, separate from OPNAV and not subordinate to the CNO. The CNO could only influence its deliberations and decisions indirectly, by preparing studies for the board's consideration and by sending witnesses to the board's confidential hearings.[13] Once King became COMINCH/CNO, he created the Ships Characteristics Board within OPNAV and made it responsible for reviewing ship plans drawn up by the Bureau of Ships. Although the General Board survived King's tenure, it never regained its prewar influence. The bond between OPNAV and the Bureau of Ships was too strong by 1945 to be broken.

Another sign of OPNAV's growing importance was the fact that many of the Navy's most respected young flag officers took OPNAV posts in 1946-1947: Arthur W. Radford (OP-05), Forrest P. Sherman (OP-03), Louis E. Denfeld (OP-01), Richard L. Conolly (OP-02), Robert B. Carney (OP-04), and William H. P. Blandy (OP-06).[14] Radford later became Chairman of the Joint Chiefs of Staff; Denfeld, Sherman, and Carney were eventually appointed Chiefs of Naval Operations; Conolly and Blandy were serious candidates for the CNO's post.

The issue of OPNAV's optimal structure was never really resolved after the war. There were too many other things to do. Congress wanted to institutionalize the lessons of the war; President Truman wanted to unify the services; and the Joint Chiefs and the services were concerned about the possible military threats from the Soviet Union. Strategic issues overshadowed the need to reorganize OPNAV. In January 1947, for example, the Navy's part of joint war plan Pincher called for conventional attacks by carrier aircraft on Soviet submarines in their bases. The Russian threat appeared to be basically one of submarine attacks on ships linking the United States to Europe and Asia. That same December, however, the Assistant Chief of Naval Operations for Guided Missiles argued in a memo to the CNO that the Navy could and should compete head-to-head with the newly created Air Force for the mission of strategic nuclear bombing.[15] Just what were the proper Navy missions? With changes in technology, Navy roles and capabilities were a matter of debate, even within the Navy.

Truman had submitted defense reorganization proposals to Congress in 1946, but Army and Navy officers called to testify before Congress clearly disagreed on the proper shape of any future higher organization for defense. The lack of consensus between the two major services kept any significant reorganization proposal from gaining wide support. Secretary Forrestal had been discussing reorganization proposals with Secretary of War Robert Patterson even before the President approached Congress. The two service secretaries finally agreed in May 1946 that there should be no single armed service chief of staff and that the Navy would keep the Marines and the aviation forces necessary for seagoing operations. In November 1946 Major General Lauris Norstad, Army Director of Plans and Operations, began working with Vice Admiral Sherman, DCNO for Operations, on the issue of service unification. Sherman convinced Norstad to accept the proposals first presented to Forrestal by the secretary's friend and advisor Ferdinand Eberstadt in September 1945, and those proposals were later incorporated into the National Security Act.

In July 1947 Congress passed the National Security Act (Public Law 253), creating a National Military Establishment of three executive departments (Army, Navy, and Air Force) under the general direction of a Secretary of Defense. The law also created the National Security Council (NSC) and the Central Intelligence Agency (CIA). The Joint Chiefs of Staff were given statutory legitimacy and charged with developing strategic plans and providing for the "strategic direction of the military forces," as well as preparing "joint logistic plans," "policies for joint training," and " policies for coordinating the education of members of the military forces."[16] The law also gave the JCS a joint staff of no more that one hundred officers. Finally, the National Security Act set forth the combat roles of the armed services, touching off a disagreement between the Navy and the Air Force that would lead to a national political crisis in October 1949.

Even before Congress had passed the National Security Act, however, the President appointed an Air Policy Commission to develop an "integrated national aviation policy."[17] Congress established its own joint Aviation Policy Board that same month (July 1947), and the two groups considered the same set of problems. In January 1948 the President's commission issued its report, arguing that the nation's defense and its defense organization had to "be built around the air arm."[18] The congressional panel argued that the first objective of any future war would be "the industrial organization and the resources of the enemy."[19] President Truman considered the report of the Air Policy Commission so politically charged that he delayed making it public until the day after he submitted the Fiscal Year 1949 budget, the first with joint figures for the three services.[20]

Tension among the services—especially between the Air Force and the

Navy—grew worse in 1948. In March, Forrestal, who now held the new post of Secretary of Defense, called the service chiefs to Key West, Florida, to clear up the debate about service roles and missions—a debate that the National Security Act of 1947 had not ended. The resulting agreements, entitled "Functions of the Armed Forces and the Joint Chiefs of Staff," promulgated by Forrestal in April, spelled out in some detail the areas of responsibility of each service.[21] The service chiefs also used the meetings in Key West to press Truman to ask Congress for a restoration of conscription, which he did.

The Key West agreements did not end the battle in the press and in the JCS between the Navy and the Air Force, however.[22] One unresolved issue was the question, Which service (if any) would be the executive agent for the JCS in the area of strategic nuclear weapons? The issue stemmed from the limited supply of nuclear raw material. Only one service would be assigned responsibility for the small number of weapons. The Air Force wanted sole responsibility for strategic nuclear weapons, but Forrestal had already approved Navy plans to construct a large carrier equipped with aircraft that could carry atomic bombs. Air Force plans to organize and control strategic air warfare seemed threatened by Navy claims that carrier-based bombers had a better chance of surviving Russian air defenses than the heavy land-based bombers of SAC.

In August 1948 Forrestal called the service chiefs together in Newport, Rhode Island, in an effort to resolve the dispute over which service would be the agent for the Joint Chiefs in controlling strategic nuclear air warfare. The service chiefs agreed that strategic air warfare would indeed be the responsibility of the Air Force, but they also agreed that the Air Force had to accept whatever strategic capability the Navy carriers could offer.[23]

Congress responded to the President's call for conscription, by passing the Selective Service Act of 1948. As Robert Connery observed in his study of industrial mobilization, in addition to providing for conscription the law "empowered the President, through the head of any government agency, to use a mandatory order on any manufacturer or producer for supplies or services when necessary for defense."[24] It was, as Forrestal knew, one step toward rearming the nation for a possible confrontation with the Soviet Union. Forrestal, however, was moving away from his previous opposition to a strong Defense secretary heading a unified department. That caused Navy officers to fear yet another attempt at unification. Their fears seemed confirmed by Forrestal's decision in May 1948 to unify Army and Navy aviation transport organizations in the Military Air Transport Service. Senior Navy officers who opposed the consolidation interpreted Forrestal's decision as the beginning of a process that would gradually strip the Navy of its less central components until it was forced to rely on support from the Air Force and the Army. As historian David Rosenberg noted, "Misunderstanding and conflict between the services was worse by the fall of 1948 than it had been before passage of the National Security Act a year before."[25]

Secretary of Defense Forrestal appeared to be behaving more like an enemy, and the uniformed Navy felt compelled to develop its own response to the pressures from the Air Force and from the advocates of a centrally managed Defense Department. In 1946 CNO Nimitz had created a General Planning Group in the Office of the Vice Chief of Naval Operations to coordinate the actions of the Deputy Chiefs of Naval Operations.[26] This organization helped the deputy chiefs coordinate their strategic planning, but it was not prepared for the interservice struggles that marked 1948 and 1949. Admiral Louis Denfeld, Nimitz's successor, turned to the General Board for long-range plans in 1947, and later, in December 1948, created in OPNAV the Organizational Research and Policy Division (OP-23), the successor to Forrestal's Committee on Research on Reorganization. The head of the new division, Captain Arleigh Burke, who was charged with countering arguments favoring service unification, eventually became one of the most articulate spokesmen for the Navy's views on defense organization.

Burke was just in time to land in the middle of major flap over defense policy and organization. In March 1949 President Truman forced Forrestal from office and appointed Louis A. Johnson, a "quarrelsome, efficient, and ambitious executive," and a former Assistant Secretary of War, as Secretary of Defense.[27] Johnson promptly cancelled

K-5155 U.S. Air Force

Secretary of Defense Louis A. Johnson and the armed services secretaries hold a press conference, 29 March 1949. *Left to right*: Secretary of the Air Force Stuart Symington, Secretary of the Army Kenneth C. Royall, Secretary Johnson, and Secretary of the Navy John L. Sullivan.

construction of the Navy's supercarrier *United States* on the grounds that the newly created North Atlantic Alliance gave the Strategic Air Command access to bases in England from which its bombers could reach targets within the Soviet Union. Publicly, Johnson claimed that the country could not afford such large ships and their accompanying air groups. With the cancellation, Secretary of the Navy John L. Sullivan resigned. Captain Burke warned CNO Denfeld that Johnson would eventually try to shift naval aviation to the Air Force and the Marines to the Army.[28]

In his work as director of OP-23, Burke gave voice to the Navy's command tradition in statements and papers for OPNAV spokesmen to use in public appearances and presentations to Congress. In March 1949, in a memo to CNO Denfeld, Burke argued that the advantage of the National Military Establishment, created by the National Security Act of 1947, was that it divided and balanced the powers of military leadership, thereby preventing rash action—a real possibility if military leadership were concentrated in one individual or organization. Burke's point was that a division of power among coequal services was essential to preserve civilian authority. He also refused to accept the contention that divided powers in the hands of multiple service chiefs led to waste and inefficiency.[29]

In an August memo to Vice Admiral Carney, Burke opposed any moves to increase the authority of the Navy Comptroller and the Management Engineer, both uniformed officers who advised the Secretary of the Navy. About the latter, Burke wrote: "The change of the Management Engineer from an advisory position to one where he exercises *functional* control over Bureaus and Offices in effect clothes him with responsibilities which have traditionally been reserved for command." He objected to giving the comptroller authority over Navy officers "because unless the Comptroller were a line officer, a civilian or a staff corps officer would be exercising authority in the purely military sphere. On the other hand, if the Comptroller is a line officer, he will be functioning in a field which has heretofore been reserved as the province of the civilian executive assistants to the Secretary." Burke argued further that a strong comptroller's office might "provide a stronger impetus for the creation of a Departmental General Staff."[30]

In September, in a memo for the Chairman of the General Board on "the Applicability of the General Staff System to the Navy," Burke admitted:

> The merger controversy found the Navy with no firm objective of its own, and no firm ideas as to how to combat a concept which the Navy . . . found undesirable. This lack of naval objective was in part, at least, a result of there being incomplete naval recognition of the political function of a national service headquarters.[31]

In other words, OPNAV had two basic responsibilities: to plan and prepare for war, and to deal with political threats external to the Navy. Burke's ideas both built on and rejected the Navy's tradition of command. Burke endorsed the concept of civilian control, but only if and when that control respected the military chain of command. In this regard he was very traditional. At the same time, however, Burke placed the duty of understanding and manipulating the Navy's external environment on uniformed military officers in OPNAV. That was *not* traditional at all. Carney gave the reason for the break with tradition in another memo for the General Board:

> The Air Force labored under great difficulties as a part of the Army and was often forced into paths of circuitousness and rebellion to achieve its proper place in the sun. Many now in key positions in the Air Force are men who participated in their Revolution, and their general approach to their problems still reflects their personal experiences.[32]

Burke took the same view—that conspiratorial organizational tactics, coupled with adroit public relations techniques, were for the Air Force legitimate tools to get what it wanted. The Navy had to respond—with or without leadership from the civilian Secretary of the Navy and his assistants.

Burke made his views clear in "Trends in Unification," a memo prepared on 16 October 1949, *after* CNO Denfeld had testified before the House Armed Services Committee hearings on the unification controversy in opposition to the views of Secretary of the Navy Francis P. Matthews. Denfeld's testimony led to his dismissal, and Burke's memo carried some of the bitterness felt within OPNAV toward the whole unification issue. Burke argued that there was a trend toward robbing the Navy of its ability to fulfill the functions assigned it by law.

> First, constant pressure is exerted toward the reassignment and redistribution of . . . the roles and missions of the armed forces. Second, continuing efforts are being made to reduce, either by budgetary action, executive order, or statutory proposals, the forces of the Navy. . . . Third, there is an obvious trend in the field of organization and management toward greater centralization of control over the three military departments.[33]

As Burke put it, the Navy supported "the principle of decentralized operation under authoritative policy direction," but the cumulative effect of postwar changes in law and administration was to undermine that principle.[34]

The story of the passage of the amendments to the National Security

Act, approved by Congress on 10 August 1949, is told elsewhere, as is the struggle between the Navy and the Air Force over the B-36 bomber.[35] What is important is the way in which the Navy's leadership interpreted actions taken in the name of "efficiency," or in the name of improving cooperation among the services. Naval leaders regarded them as part of an overall strategy to destroy the Navy and its tradition of decentralized command. The OP-23 October memo expressed this view: "The many developments, of course, are being undertaken separately and without any outward acknowledgment of interrelationship. Yet viewed as a whole they bear striking resemblance to a pattern of military development described by General Heinz Guderian, Hitler's last Chief of Staff."[36] The issue was not one of budgets or resources or careers.

> The ultimate development . . . appears to be the establishment of a supreme general staff to coordinate all military functions with a subordinate "armed forces office" to manage such non-combat functions as procurement, medical service, personnel policy, recruiting, and research. The individual services, then, would be reduced virtually to technical branches of the military establishment.[37]

These memos portrayed the struggle over service unification and service roles more as one over ideas than over resources. Although they rarely admitted it, Burke and other officers involved in the controversy were debating constitutional principles. They were arguing about the proper role and organization of military leadership. For Burke, the chief duty of a CNO was political—to represent the Navy at the highest levels of the executive branch and in Congress, where the fundamental battles over authority and responsibility were fought. Burke believed that the Army and Air Force neither understood nor accepted the Navy's unique tradition of executive leadership. Indeed, the October memo suggested that the Navy's view on the distribution of authority was in fact the more proper one—the more constitutionally correct one. But the Air Force, clearly, did not see matters that way, which forced the Navy to wage a partisan struggle to preserve what it considered to be the proper, or constitutional, relationship between military and civilian powers.

Burke strongly opposed any efforts to consolidate service activities because he believed all such efforts were motivated by a kind of misguided ideology. In his view, terms like "efficiency" and "jointness" were used in congressional hearings to disguise attacks on the Navy. The Navy's task was to deflect and defeat both the ideologues and the well-intentioned, but misinformed, politicians. When Forrestal was Navy secretary, the Navy had a civilian champion for its cause. By October 1949, OP-23 was arguing that the uniformed service leadership had to do what the secretary's office would not. The CNO, then, was as much a political and constitutional warrior as an operational commander.

OP-23's arguments in 1949 formed the basis for the Navy's later positions toward the Joint Chiefs of Staff and the Defense Department. The Navy suspected that both institutions were following a long-term strategy to strip the Navy of its independence and to overcentralize the military leadership of the country. OP-23 memos presented an argument familiar to readers of James Madison's Federalist Paper No. 10: competition among factions (in this case the services) was beneficial because it allowed civilians both to retain control of the military and to consider alternative national military strategies. Burke carried that view, to which many Navy officers subscribed, with him into office when he became CNO in 1955. Indeed, it is still a widely held, if sometimes not well-argued, position among senior Navy officers.

Admiral Forrest Sherman, Nimitz's Deputy Chief of Staff for Plans during the last two years of the war, replaced Denfeld as CNO. Sherman, reputedly one of the best strategic minds in Washington, had represented the Navy in talks with the Army when the services developed the outlines for the National Security Act of 1947. Building on his reputation and on his contacts in the other services, he acted quickly to restore service morale and to gain friends and allies for the Navy. As Rosenberg noted, Sherman's positive "impact was felt almost immediately."[38]

Before Secretary of Defense Johnson cancelled construction of the supercarrier *United States* and fired Denfeld in October 1949, the Air Warfare Division (OP-55) in the Office of the DCNO for Air had produced (that August) a new study that justified large aircraft carriers. In 1947 Navy planners perceived the Soviet threat as one primarily of submarines at sea. They had accordingly advocated carrier air strikes as a means of striking Soviet submarines at their bases before they could slip into the Atlantic and Pacific and prowl the shipping lanes linking the United States and its European and Asian clients. In 1949 naval aviators, as reflected in the OPNAV study, decided that Soviet air forces posed the greater immediate threat, especially to U.S. naval forces deployed in the Mediterranean. To overcome such land-based air forces, Navy carrier groups needed large numbers of high-performance aircraft to attack Soviet air bases.[39] As Friedman noted, "sea control and power projection were associated, rather than opposed, naval missions."[40] The OP-55 study was important because it provided a justification for large aircraft carriers that was *not* based on plans for staging nuclear strikes against the Soviets. Consequently, it did not add fuel to the fire generated by the B-36 controversy.

Gradually, under Sherman, the tension between the Air Force and the Navy declined, and the Navy began conceptualizing the missions that it only adopted in the late 1950s and early 1960s: using the mobility and striking potential of naval forces — especially carrier air groups able to deliver conventional and tactical nuclear ordnance — to deter or respond to threats from Soviet or Soviet-client forces in areas distant from the dividing line between NATO and the Warsaw Pact.

Soviet actions and heavy-handedness in 1949 indirectly helped all the services. By detonating an atomic weapon and trumpeting the defeat of Chiang Kai-shek as the beginning of the end of the capitalist world, the Soviet Union spurred U.S. policymakers into reassessing their attitudes toward military spending. The result was National Security Council Study 68, reviewed by President Truman in April 1950 and approved by him that September, while fighting raged in Korea. NSC-68 was the beginning of a program to increase military expenditures, especially on conventional forces. The Korean War brought more money to the services, along with (in 1953) tactical nuclear weapons and the programs to produce thermonuclear explosives. It also tested the postwar military command structure. Perhaps most importantly, Korea helped Army general and former NATO commander Dwight Eisenhower win the presidency.

3

The Eisenhower Years

The Eisenhower years were a time of great change for the Navy. The new President was neither satisfied with the existing level of service cooperation (as demonstrated in Korea) nor impressed with the ability of the JCS to link the President with his theater military commanders. He wanted to strengthen the hand of civilian defense officials and to streamline the national military command system. And in 1953 he went to Congress with proposals to do just that. Eisenhower's initiative and his strong views on national strategy led to the creation of the doctrine called the "New Look," less accurately termed "massive retaliation." By the summer of 1953 the relative cost of making nuclear weapons had drastically declined, while their versatility had dramatically improved. The question was, Could the United States use its superior nuclear weapons technology to support NATO, deter the Communist Chinese in the Far East, and reduce the reliance on large conventional forces?

The answer, reached through close consultation with the Joint Chiefs, was yes, and the services considered means to adapt their forces and skills to the requirements of strategic and tactical nuclear warfare. The Navy, for example, began developing the forces to deploy tactical nuclear weapons against submarines, supplementing its existing arsenal of weapons for use against submarine bases. The emphasis on nuclear warfare enhanced Eisenhower's already deep interest in altering the highest levels of national security administration. As the Soviet Union developed its own nuclear strategic forces, the U.S. Government would have to be prepared to respond to any swift surprise attack. Accordingly, Eisenhower went back to Congress in 1958 to ask for more changes in the laws governing national security decision making.

Eisenhower had campaigned on a platform that called for defense reorganization, and after his victory in the 1952 elections, he asked prominent Republican Nelson Rockefeller to chair a committee of experts who would suggest a list of reforms.[1] The Rockefeller Committee was guided by four objectives: to make the lines of "authority and responsibility" within the Defense Department "clear and unmistakable"; to give the Secretary of Defense the responsibility for clarifying "the roles and missions of the services"; to make planning effective by using "our modern scientific and industrial resources"; and "to effect maximum economies without injuring military strength and its necessary productive support."[2] In its April 1953 report the committee recommended the following:

• "The direction, authority, and control of the Secretary over all agencies of the Department, including the three military departments, . . . should be confirmed by decisive administrative action, and if necessary by statutory amendment."

• "The Secretaries of the military departments, subject to the direction, authority, and control of the Secretary of Defense, should be the operating heads of their respective departments in all aspects, military and civilian alike."

• "The command function" should be removed "from the Joint Chiefs of Staff, in order to enable them to work more effectively as a unified planning agency."

• The Secretary of Defense, not the Joint Chiefs, should decide which military department should serve as the executive agent for a unified command.

• The Secretary of Defense should be "free to adjust from time to time the assignment of staff functions within his own office in a flexible and expeditious manner." The assistant secretaries "should not be in the direct line of administrative authority between" the secretary "and the three military departments."

• The Joint Munitions Board and Research and Development Board created by the National Security Act of 1947 should be dissolved and their functions transferred to Assistant Secretaries of Defense.[3]

On the basis of these recommendations, Eisenhower submitted Reorganization Plan 6 to Congress at the end of April. Minor opposition to the President's proposals failed to block his suggested reforms. Consequently, the joint boards were broken up and their functions were transferred to the Office of the Secretary of Defense. The Defense secretary was allowed to appoint an additional six assistant secretaries and a general counsel. The JCS and the service chiefs were removed from the chain of command, which ran from the President to the unified and specified commanders, and replaced by the service secretaries. The Chairman of the Joint Chiefs was authorized to review appointments to the Joint Staff and to manage the staff.[4]

DOD Directive 5158.1 of 26 July 1954 implemented Eisenhower's reorganization proposals. Perhaps the most important part of the directive was the first statement under the "Implementation" section: "The Joint Staff work of each of the Chiefs of Staff shall take priority over all other duties."[5] Part 6 of that section read, "Development of strategic and logistic plans will be based on the broadest conceptions of over-all national interest rather than the special desires of a particular service."[6] The President, displeased with the way he believed the Joint Chiefs had functioned during the Second World War, now directed the service chiefs to focus their time and energy on joint issues through an institution that had adequate staff support and that was tied closely to the Office of the Secretary of Defense.

The Defense Cataloging and Standardization Act, passed by Congress in 1953, had created a single, standard catalog for the Defense Supply Management Agency to use when it procured material for all three services. DOD Directive 5158.1 abolished the Defense Supply Management Agency, but did not shift the agency's functions back to the services. Instead, the authority to procure common articles was given to the Secretary of Defense, who was empowered to create "single manager" agencies in procurement areas such as clothing, medical supplies, petroleum products, and food. Nearly twenty years later, Navy logisticians would interpret this act as the beginning of a tug-of-war between the services and the Secretary of Defense that the latter would eventually win.

Secretary of the Navy Robert B. Anderson responded to congressional acceptance of Reorganization Plan 6 by appointing Under Secretary of the Navy Thomas S. Gates, Jr., to head a special study committee to consider the Navy's organization. The Gates Committee struggled with the problem of how to give the Secretary of the Navy administrative control over the department without diluting the CNO's authority on the Joint Chiefs of Staff. If the CNO, as a member of the JCS, had access to the Defense secretary and the President, then was he subordinate to the Navy secretary? And, if the Navy secretary were in fact the "manager" of the Navy Department, then did he need special access to OPNAV for information and reports necessary to monitor the department's performance? Moreover, if the Secretary of the Navy could authorize the CNO to act for him, then was the CNO still as powerful as he had been before Reorganization Plan 6? Finally, there was the problem of time. After Reorganization Plan 6, both the Secretary of the Navy and the CNO seemed to have additional duties that were not easily delegated. How could the OPNAV and Secretariat staffs best support the managerial and decision-making responsibilities of their leaders?

To answer these questions, the Gates Committee went back to basics. First, it considered the three general orders from the Navy Secretariat which distributed authority and responsibility within the department: Number 5, which covered the administration of the department; Number 9, which specified the organization of the Navy's operating forces; and Number 19, which covered the shore activities of the department. Then the committee reviewed the basic structure of the Naval Establishment—the Navy Department and its bureaus, the operating forces, and the shore support facilities—observing that it was a divided, decentralized organization. The bureaus, for example, reported to the Secretary of the Navy, but were supposed to satisfy the requirements set by OPNAV for weapons, training, and personnel, so there was a dual chain of command within the Navy Department itself. The CNO was subordinate to the Secretary of the Navy, but the secretary did not participate in the deliberations of the Joint Chiefs, and traditionally did not interfere in the CNO's command of the operating forces (a heritage of the Second World War). The CNO organized the "consumer" side of the Navy so that the "producer" side—the bureaus—could develop programs to meet the present and future needs of the operating forces in areas such as weapons and weapons platforms.

What held the whole Naval Establishment together, according to the committee, was ongoing consultation among Navy leaders. As the committee observed in its report, "many working level committees and groups are dealing with specific technical and management areas."[7] But the committee also noted that only two such committees were "concerned with top level problems," so "more effective coordination of all aspects of operation and management of the department would result from the establishment of a group of internal advisory committees made up of key executives and designed to deal with specific categories of problems."[8] The Navy's two high-level coordinating committees were the Navy Management Council, chaired by the under secretary and consisting of senior military and civilian Navy officials, and a weekly conclave of the bureau chiefs, which met under the auspices of the assistant secretary. The Gates Committee recommended that the secretary create six senior-level groups for general department policy, material procurement, Navy facilities and base construction, personnel policy, reserve forces, and for research and development.

The Gates Committee also proposed that the Navy secretary act as congressional liaison, coordinate public relations and relations with the Office of the Secretary of Defense, and supervise the "producer logistics segment" of the department through the under secretary. The committee recommended making the seven bureaus and other assistants to the secretary "accountable" to the under secretary "for total performance." Gates and his colleagues also advocated giving the under secretary an office of analysis and review, which would prepare "consolidated statistical and analytical performance appraisals of each important program." Other recommendations included:

• Designating an Assistant Secretary of the Navy for Financial Management—a comptroller;

• Making the Assistant Secretary of the Navy responsible for "policy, management and control of production, procurement, supply, distribution and maintenance of material";

• Coordinating the Navy's "producer logistics" by the Under Secretary of the Navy through the assistant secretaries (especially Assistant Secretary for Material) and the bureaus;

• Relieving the Assistant Secretary for Air of his personnel powers, but giving him responsibility "for policy, management and control of functions relating to aeronautical matters (except those aspects concerned with producer logistics under the cognizance of the other Assistant Secretaries), and for Research and Development"; and

• Designating a new Assistant Secretary for Personnel and Reserve Forces, with responsibility "for policy, management and control of functions relating to personnel . . . and matters relating to policy and administration of public housing and quarters."[9]

The Gates Committee deliberations attempted to balance the new duties of the Secretary of the Navy and the CNO with the Navy's traditional, decentralized form of management. The proposals to create committees, which would determine the policies of the Naval Establishment, avoided giving too much authority to individuals, but still created institutional settings where these same individuals could and would act jointly to set policy. The basic reform of Reorganization Plan 6, which placed the service secretaries directly in the chain of command, caused severe administrative problems because it gave both the Navy secretary and the CNO access to the Defense secretary and the President without clearly dividing their respective duties. The committee tried to avoid head-to-head conflicts and to encourage consensus by creating joint administrative boards.

The changes did not succeed. While Secretary of the Navy Anderson delegated authority to Admiral Carney, Chief of Naval Operations (1953–1955), his successor, Charles S. Thomas, was more jealous of his prerogatives. Carney also irritated Secretary of Defense Charles Wilson when he communicated directly—as service chiefs were authorized to do—with the President. It was not clear whether Carney or Thomas was the principal naval advisor to the President. Finally, the CNO had to deal with a very assertive and capable senior admiral, Arthur Radford, Chairman of the Joint Chiefs and a very powerful advocate of long-range strategic bombing. As historian Paul Schratz pointed out, Admiral Radford "retained tremendous influence within the Navy Department and he actively cultivated the support of Secretary of the Navy Thomas, who soon fell under his sway."[10] The connection between Thomas and

Radford, and Carney's strong insistence on his command and presidential advisory prerogatives as CNO (codified in Public Law 432 of 5 March 1948), kept the Gates Committee's proposals for collegial leadership committees from ever getting off the ground.

Carney, however, did heed the committee's call for improved institutional planning and DOD Directive 5158.1's instruction that the services work closer with the Joint Chiefs and the Defense secretary. In April 1954 he set up an ad hoc group to consider future shipbuilding plans and programs. The following year, in February 1955, he established the Long Range Objectives Group (OP-93) to consider major Navy programs ten to fifteen years into the future.[11] To enable the CNO to serve as an effective member of the Joint Chiefs, Carney placed the responsibility for JCS matters and strategic planning in a new office, the Deputy Chief of Naval Operations for Plans and Policy (OP-06). OP-06's predecessor in the area of joint military policy and planning was the DCNO for Operations (OP-03). The changes in defense organization initiated by President Eisenhower required Admiral Carney to change OPNAV's organization so that the Navy would not be outmaneuvered in competition at the JCS level. He said later:

> As CNO and a member of the JCS I was under pressure to defend Navy interests against Army/Air Force proposals to preempt the major theater and unified commands. My staff spent too much time in defensive effort. Curiously, my combat-proven deputy was reluctant to generate comparable power-grab proposals, typical of a widespread mentality that was basically conservative, honest—and, I thought, naive.[12]

The Gates Committee had responded to Reorganization Plan 6 by trying to strengthen the Secretariat so that it could fulfill its new, mandated responsibilities. Admiral Carney responded to Plan 6 by becoming more aggressive in the Navy Department and in the JCS. He perceived that the plan left more authority in the hands of the service secretaries than the average civilian appointee could handle. Carney also realized that the New Look, which Admiral Radford had helped to shape for the President, had major long-range implications. The same question was asked again: what mission would the Navy have if the nation's major strategy were a nuclear one? The Navy needed strong representation in the JCS, and that representation required a staff capable of dealing with strategic issues. Carney acted to build OP-06 as a competent link to and a shield against the JCS. He also started a process of long-range planning to give the CNO some warning of future military and technological developments that would affect the Navy's strategic role.

In mid-1955, after Secretary Thomas decided not to ask for Admiral

CNO Burke on a visit to the Mediterranean addresses the crew of destroyer *Waller* (DD–466).

NH 67921

Carney's reappointment, President Eisenhower appointed Rear Admiral Arleigh Burke the Chief of Naval Operations. If the President and Secretary of Defense Wilson ever thought that Burke was less likely to resist defense reorganization than Carney, they were in for a surprise. Indeed, Burke himself told the Senate before his confirmation that he had not abandoned the positions that he had presented so forcefully in 1949, when he was head of OP–23. As the President and the other services would learn, Burke meant what he said.

As CNO, Burke was a energetic administrator and a shrewd leader. He moved quickly to win the support of OPNAV and the Navy by retaining Carney's "entire immediate staff," by consulting with the Navy's senior commanders in the Atlantic and Pacific, and by personally writing a monthly newsletter for flag officers.[13] As he earned the support of officers senior to him in service, Burke began a process of giving the Navy a principal role in Eisenhower's New Look strategy. In October 1955 Burke pursued a joint project with the Army to put an IRBM to sea. When the solid-fueled Polaris missile was developed, the Navy pursued its program separately from the Army, eventually placing Polaris on nuclear-powered submarines. He also initiated a study of Navy organization, appointing Vice Admiral Ruthven E. Libby chairman of a special board of inquiry "to study and report upon the adequacy of the Bureau System of organization." Burke believed that the Navy's future was in jeopardy, and he wanted to make sure that his service was organized to stay at the cutting edge of military technology.

Burke convened the Libby Board because he and other senior officers were concerned about the lack of success of the Navy's antiair missile program—the three "Ts" (Terrier, Tartar, and Talos missiles). Shifting the surface Navy from guns to missiles took longer than planned, but it was an essential move because existing middle- and short-range antiaircraft guns were inadequate against modern jet aircraft. Moreover, the fact that those aircraft could carry nuclear weapons meant that they had to be engaged at the longest ranges practicable. The basic idea behind the three "T" program was to build a layered air defense around Navy formations, with missiles of different ranges engaging attacking aircraft as they flew closer to the center of the U.S. formation. The idea was sound, but getting the new weapons into the fleet took longer than anticipated. Burke wanted to know if the problem was an engineering or organizational one.[14]

In his letter of instruction to the board, Burke observed:

> Weapons and weapons systems are becoming more and more complicated, with more and more interdependent components. Interest in, and in some cases, cognizance of certain of these components, is common to the three so-called material bureaus, as a result of which constant interchange of information and constant coordination is required.[15]

The question was whether this constant exchange and coordination was being done properly. In March 1956 the Libby Board issued its report. Classified at the time, it first summarized the developmental process and then suggested changes. The key to the developmental process in the Navy was the generation of "operational requirements," or statements of "*what*, *when*, and *where* of desired specific systems or equipment."[16] As the report declared:

> Nowhere in the present system is there provision specifically for performing the function of conceiving, in general physical terms, new weapon systems and system complexes *which relate to the entire field of naval warfare*. . . .
>   Such system development planning as is going on now is fragmentized among the several warfare desks [in OPNAV]. . . . Thus the systems here developed tend to be entities within their own operational categories;

1116848 U.S. Navy

The Terrier surface-to-air missile system on board attack aircraft carrier *America* (CVA-66).

K-39498 U.S. Navy

Talos missiles on board guided missile cruiser *Columbus* (CG-12).

> no one agency correlates the systems between or among categories; and no one agency is charged with coordinating all the systems with their essential logistic support.[17]

But the board was uncomfortable with the suggestion that the bureaus of Ordnance, Aeronautics, and Ships be given certain areas of absolute technical dominance. Its report observed that "it has been impossible to arrive at a determination of Bureau cognizance" in missile design and development "because the development of almost any guided missile system requires the specialized skills and capabilities of more than one bureau."[18] Indeed, two successful missile designs—the Sidewinder air-to-air missile and the Regulus surface-to-surface cruise missile—emerged from bureaus (Ordnance and Aeronautics, respectively) whose primary duties did not cover those types of weapons. The board suggested that the CNO establish a conceptual weapons systems group in OPNAV. Board members wanted to preserve the bureau system and opposed using special "task forces" to develop new weapons, just as they voted against "arbitrary and rigid assignment of cognizance over an entire weapon system."[19]

Yet the Libby Board placed the initiative for new systems development in OPNAV rather than with the bureaus. Praising a study on long-range shipbuilding ordered by former CNO Carney, the board endorsed the establishment of the Long Range Objectives Group (OP-93). Board members also supported Admiral Burke's decision to form a special Naval Warfare Analyses Group (NAVWAG), composed of both civilian and military analysts, to support OP-93.[20] In so doing, they were admitting that the traditional system of training line officers as ordnance or aviation specialists and alternating them between the fleet and the bureaus was not working effectively.

Organizational differences between the bureaus of Ordnance and Aeronautics and the Bureau of Ships had always existed. The latter was managed more by uniformed specialists (later called Engineering Duty Only officers) who followed career paths different from those of line officers. Ordnance and Aeronautics were dominated by line officers who, because of their abilities, received postgraduate training in ballistics, engineering, or chemistry and then shuttled back and forth from the operating forces to their bureaus. Burke had been trained as an ordnance officer, and many of the Naval Academy's most outstanding graduates were guided into postgraduate ordnance work before the Second World War. That tradition marked the origins of the prejudice toward the Navy's "Gun Club," or the ordnance-trained line officers, who before the war had been singled out by their superiors for outstanding careers. This system of giving qualified line officers special training leading to career advantages was defended on the grounds that it promoted communication between the operating forces, the bureaus, and the latest advances in applied science. The Libby Board's report was the first sign that this pattern of special training might not be adequate for the missile age.

The board also suggested that the CNO direct newer, complex systems development because the task of generating operational requirements was too important to be left to the various warfare desks in offices like OP-05 (Air). Burke used the force of the recommendation to justify his decision to ask the Secretary of the Navy to create a Special Projects Office to develop the Polaris missile and its platform, or platforms. Burke placed a special board, with senior civilian and Navy members, over the new organization and gave the Special Projects Office first priority in funding and staffing. It was the Navy's bootstrap effort to make a place for itself in the strategic missile forces and it worked. Rosenberg characterized Burke's strong, unswerving support for the Special Projects Office as "probably the single most significant action of his six years as chief of naval operations."[21] The significant point, however, was that Burke refused to accept the Air Force claim to primacy in the strategic field, and he took control of the planning processes in OPNAV in order to carry on that fight with the Air Force.

The Libby Board also recommended that the Secretary of the Navy establish an Inter-Bureau Technical Group and an Executive Council (with bureau representation) for Development and Production. It also endorsed the concept of the "lead bureau," whereby OPNAV would give coordinating authority to a bureau in a particular area of development, such as surface-to-air missiles. The Navy's shift from guns to missiles, and then from analog to digital technology, had caused the coordination problems among the major bureaus. So long as sensors, such as radar, remained relatively simple (and inexpensive) and missiles had little influence on ship and aircraft designs, coordination problems were limited. Systems could be added to, or subtracted from, basic hull and powerplant designs with simple modifications. The difficulty arose when the missiles and their sensors and guidance systems began to dominate surface ship and aircraft design. Platform designers were on the edge of a revolution—integrated ship and aircraft systems design— and the bureaus had to rethink their accepted boundaries.

The process would not be easy. Navy leaders wanted the bureaus to be centers of applied expertise and the Navy's laboratories to be centers of research and innovation. But rapid advances in technology required a stronger technical education for line officers and constant retraining. At the same time bureau personnel wanted assurance that their chosen careers would last; they did not want to make a commitment to naval engineering and development and then lose their jobs when a new technology replaced the old. In the nuclear submarine program, for example, Admiral Rickover had solved the problem of training and holding skilled personnel by fostering simultaneously military and civilian technology. The one nourished the other. The Navy supplied trained operators for the civilian nuclear power program, while the civilian manufacturers maintained development efforts to benefit the Navy. There were dangers in this close military/civilian relationship, however. On the one hand, the military risked losing control of the direction of technology. On the other, if the Navy retained control by freezing design development, it risked missing technological opportunities. These dangers were not apparent either to Burke or to the Libby Board in 1956, but were realized by the late 1970s.

4

Burke: Shielding the Navy

After his first two years as CNO, Burke clearly saw that President Eisenhower was not satisfied with service cooperation, joint planning, and the type of defense management allowed by existing laws. Nor was Congress. By 1957, for example, all three services were developing or producing both cruise missiles and intermediate-range ballistic missiles. This appeared to be a typical case of duplication. To reduce such apparently wasted effort, Congress wanted to give the Secretary of Defense the power to set programs, not simply package them for presentation. Congress and the President also wanted some central, unified planning for nuclear war. Outside the government, the Rockefeller Foundation had funded a series of studies on national security. One such study, completed while Admiral Burke was CNO, recommended that the service chiefs be removed from the chain of command and that the Joint Staff of the JCS be both reorganized and strengthened.[1] As it became obvious to the services that the President would submit another proposal for DOD reorganization to Congress, Burke prepared for a rerun of the unification debates. The chronology of Navy responses to the recommendations of the Rockefeller panel on defense reorganization shows how carefully Admiral Burke prepared and managed the Navy's position:

October 1957: The CNO formed a special committee in OPNAV to study the alternatives to the panel's likely recommendations. (That same month Eisenhower privately said that he favored eliminating separate military services.)

December 1957: The Deputy Chief of Naval Operations for Plans and Policy (OP-06) solicited comments within the Navy (not just within OPNAV) regarding possible changes to DOD and service organization.

January 1958: The Rockefeller reorganization report was released.

January 1958: The first DOD reorganization bill cleared the House of Representatives, and the President supported reorganization in his "State of the Union" address.

January 1958: The Office of the Secretary of Defense began a formal study of DOD organization.

February 1958: The OPNAV staff completed its study, begun in

October 1957, on the consequences of JCS control over theater operations and joint commands.

April 1958: The administration's reorganization bill was introduced in the House.

May 1958: Largely at the request of the Navy Department, Carl Vinson, Chairman of the House Armed Services Committee, introduced his own reorganization bill.

June 1958: With Senate Armed Services Committee hearings on several reorganization bills underway, Admiral Burke created the Ad Hoc Committee to Review the Navy Department Organization to consider the effects of these bills should they become law.[2]

Burke opposed all proposals to merge the military departments, to create a single chief of staff of the armed forces, and to fashion the Joint Staff into an effective general staff. He began a burdensome and time-consuming correspondence, arguing his case with influential retired flag officers. He ordered the DCNO for Plans and Policy to develop a special proposal to send to Congress for reorganizing the Office of the Secretary of Defense. He tried to dissuade President Eisenhower from submitting a bill that would strip the CNO of operational authority, and he welcomed the support of Vinson and his colleague, Representative Paul Kilday (D-Texas), the second ranking majority member of the House Armed Services Committee. Vinson and Kilday insisted that any reform legislation *not* authorize the Secretary of Defense to merge the services, or create a single chief of staff, or establish an "overall armed forces general staff."[3] Despite Burke's opposition, however, the Department of Defense Reorganization Act of 1958 did eliminate the operational authority of the service chiefs.

The new law removed the service secretaries from the chain of command; the revised chain of command ran from the President to the Secretary of Defense, through the Joint Chiefs of Staff, to the unified (such as CINCPAC) and specified (such as SAC) field commanders. The Joint Chiefs did not act as their organization's delegated representatives in the chain of command. However, the JCS advisory role was strengthened by giving the chairman a vote in their deliberations, by increasing the size of the Joint Staff, and by permitting the Joint Staff to organize along traditional staff lines and abandon the joint committee structure in use since 1947. Before 1958 the Joint Staff consisted of several major staff committees: strategic plans, intelligence, logistics, military assistance, and advanced studies. After 1958 the Joint Staff was set up along Army lines with directorates: J-1 for personnel, J-2 for intelligence, J-3 for operations, J-4 for logistics, and so forth. CNO Burke had always regarded the JCS as less a military organization than a political one in which service chiefs had to struggle for resources and authority, and he drove his staff to keep one step ahead of the other services, especially the Air Force. But the reorganization of the Joint Staff along Army lines meant an organizational philosophy that *felt* alien to Navy officers, and the Navy developed a strong prejudice against sending its best officers for joint work.[4]

What concerned Burke, however, was the increased authority that the 1958 law gave the Secretary of Defense. Subject to a veto by either house of Congress, the Secretary of Defense could alter service functions. The secretary could also reorganize the department's supply and service activities and assign new weapons systems development and use to one service. Finally, the secretary could delegate his authority to assistants, giving them responsibility for functions that he himself created. Within eight months of the law's passage, the commander of the Strategic Air Command took advantage of its provisions by requesting that SAC be given operational "control" of the Navy's Polaris submarine force then under construction.[5] As Rosenberg noted in his study of Burke's tenure as CNO, "Over the next fifteen months, Burke stubbornly fought the proposal, not only within the Joint Chiefs, but before Congress and in the

Courtesy of Naval Sea Systems Command

A Polaris fleet ballistic missile, in the first successful test of the weapon, is fired from submerged submarine *George Washington* (SSBN-598), 20 July 1960.

press."[6] Burke won that contest but lost a later debate over whether there should be a Joint Strategic Target Planning Staff with SAC's commander as its director.[7]

During the debate over defense organization in 1958, Burke asked Rear Admiral Allan L. Reed of OP-92 (Intelligence) to study OPNAV. Burke particularly wanted to know why the Navy appeared to be on the defensive in the debates over national security organization. Reed's answers, in a confidential report, were revealing.

> The habit of thinking of naval officers has always been more individualistic than that of officers in the other services. This makes for vigor in action and produces good ideas, but it . . . tends to inhibit the teamwork and support of officially stated policies and doctrines necessary in the highest staffs. . . .[8] Naval officers in general do not consider it an honor to be assigned to the Office of the Chief of Naval Operations. . . . The degree of identification with special interests such as naval aviation, the submarine service, or surface specialties tends to encourage the formation of cliques and to discourage viewpoints and thinking oriented toward the best interests of the Navy as a whole.[9]

The solution: "encourage the development within the line of the Navy of a group of officers of all ranks and branches, thoroughly trained in staff work, and qualified through experience to assist the highest commanders in the solution of problems and in formulating and implementing policy." But there was a catch, as he realized: "This is admittedly coming close to the concept of a 'General Staff Corps.'"[10]

To avoid that apostasy, Reed suggested breaking down the "distinct feeling of compartmentation" by making sure that all warfare specialties represented in OPNAV understood current Navy doctrine.[11] He argued that OPNAV organization hindered the development of a shared sense of mission because too many officers reported directly to the Chief and Vice Chief of Naval Operations instead of working together to iron out problems. Moreover, the lines of authority in OPNAV were uncertain, and Navy officers capable of exercising delegated authority were often not given it.[12] Reed advised Burke to increase the size of his *immediate* staff under the vice chief and create a "central point for the review, coordination and dissemination of policy and doctrine."[13] As part of the latter effort, Reed recommended reducing the sweeping responsibilities of the DCNO for Air (OP-05).[14]

Reed's study was important for several reasons. First, it revealed how influential the Navy's traditions and unwritten rules for success were as the Navy battled threats from both the Air Force and the Office of the Secretary of Defense. Second, it uncovered a Navy dilemma that survives to the present day. Burke considered himself and the Navy under attack by ideologues. But the obvious means of opposing his attackers—using the same kind of tactics in return—would *not* make the Navy the kind of institution that Burke argued the nation needed to resist an over concentration of military command power. That was the dilemma. Burke did not trust military ideologues, no matter what uniform they wore. Yet he admitted that opposing them successfully sometimes demanded as much theater as rational argument. Finally, the Reed study prompted Burke to consider adding responsibilities to OP-06 (Plans and Policy), and to review his own style of leadership.

The more immediate problem, however, was the response to the Department of Defense Reorganization Act of 1958. Secretary of the Navy Thomas Gates appointed a board in August 1958 to address the impact of the new law on the Navy's organization. Chaired by Under Secretary of the Navy William B. Franke, the board convened for six months before recommending the following:

• Retain the Navy's bilinear system of parallel civilian and military administration (the Secretary of the Navy and the CNO).

• Change General Orders Numbers 5 and 9 to reflect the 1958 law, which eliminated the operational command authority of the CNO.

• Reorganize the Assistant Secretaries of the Navy, appointing one each for finance, manpower, material, and research and development.

Secretary of the Navy Thomas S. Gates, Jr., 1957-1959. Earlier in his career, as Under Secretary of the Navy, Gates headed a committee studying the Navy's organization.
80-G-1036018

- Create a DCNO for research and development.

- Combine the bureaus of Ordnance and Aeronautics.[15]

To make room for the new Assistant Secretary of the Navy for Research and Development, Gates abolished the office of the Assistant Secretary for Air. He also ordered the CNO to shift aviation personnel matters from OP-05 to the Bureau of Personnel, and authorized the merger of the bureaus of Ordnance and Aeronautics.[16] (See Figure 2.)

Burke's special Ad Hoc Committee to Review the Navy Department Organization had reported in July, before the 1958 reforms became law. It recommended that OPNAV be reorganized along functional lines, with the DCNO for Air losing influence and the bureaus losing their independence. The original, uncorrected draft of the ad hoc committee's report argued that the "Chief of Naval Operations must exercise appropriate direction over Bureau operations and finances. To achieve this, the Department must bring the Bureaus and Comptroller under the Chief of Naval Operations."[17] That first draft was amended later, when the words "subject to the policy of the Secretary of the Navy" were appended to the first sentence. The Franke Board also considered subordinating the bureaus to the CNO, but it rejected the idea on the counsel of Navy line officers who worked in the bureaus.[18] Burke's committee was taking an audacious stand in recommending that the CNO, not the secretary, control the bureaus. That issue had divided former Secretary of the Navy Forrestal and former CNO Ernest King. The issue surfaced again because Burke felt pressured from the Defense secretary and indirectly from the Navy secretary. The 1958 reforms not only eliminated the operational authority of the CNO but also made the service secretaries de facto line managers for the Secretary of Defense. In that capacity, a strong Navy secretary, who was also a loyal subordinate of the Secretary of Defense, could exploit the limits on the CNO's authority to control Navy research, development, and acquisition, thereby reducing the influence of the CNO.

When the Franke Board recommended merging the bureaus of Aeronautics and Ordnance, CNO Burke began considering directors for the new organization, named the Bureau of Naval Weapons (BUWEPS). In June 1959, an OP-06 memo informed Burke that Vice Admiral Rickover, director of the Navy's nuclear propulsion program in the Bureau of Ships, had "a campaign going" to get the new position. The memo, apparently written for Burke by Captain Joseph W. Leverton, laid out a strategy for Burke to use in getting his own choice to head the new bureau.[19] The significance of the memo was that it revealed Burke's sensitivity to one of the sources of his organizational influence—his appointment authority. For example, when the 1958 DOD

OFFICE OF THE CHIEF OF NAVAL OPERATIONS, 1958

Figure 2

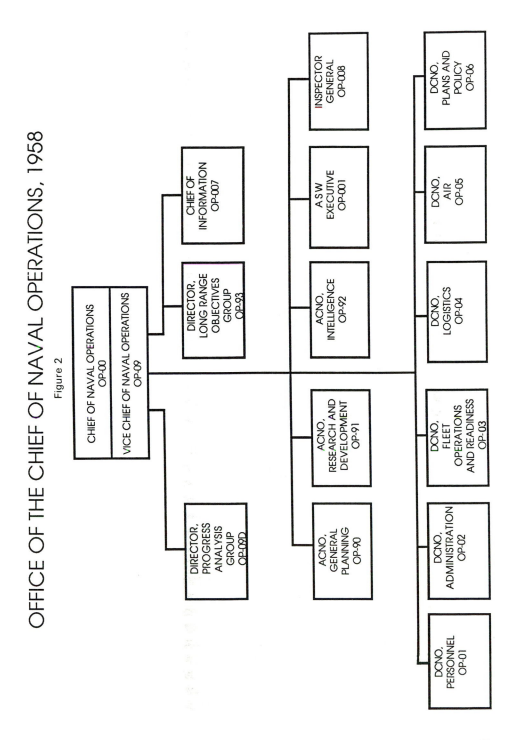

Reorganization Act was passed, the service chiefs legally lost their operational authority. Burke retained his command authority, however, by simply ignoring the 1958 law and acting as though his position was unchanged. To bolster his authority, he also relied on the need of naval component commanders in the unified commands, such as Commander in Chief, Pacific Fleet, in CINCPAC, to get the CNO's approval for reorganizations.[20] Burke understood that the CNO, through OPNAV, influenced the number and kind of billets under the component commanders. He used that influence to remind these commanders of his authority.[21]

Burke had learned to use all the resources at his disposal to shield the Navy from "misguided" outside pressure. Where he lacked resources, he relied on the strength of his personality. As the Franke Board prepared its report, for example, Burke had Captain Leverton informally solicit OPNAV personnel for impressions of Burke's managerial style. Leverton summarized his findings in two memos:

- Subordinates often did not know what the CNO expected of them.

- Burke's quick temper rubbed senior officers the wrong way.

- Subordinates felt that Burke lacked time for the really important matters because too many people with trivial issues were vying for the CNO's attention.

- Subordinates disliked Burke's habit of bypassing channels.

- Burke was seen as not delegating enough authority to his deputies.

- Despite Burke's energy and "no compromise" style, OPNAV operated like Congress: advocates of important change had to build a coalition behind their ideas through persuasion, bargaining, and compromise.

- Burke relied heavily on OP-06, ignoring other portions of OPNAV. OP-06 felt buried under work because it had to respond immediately to JCS issues.

Leverton closed by commenting that Burke's leadership style "has caused a lot of uncertainty within the staff—but it has kept them on their toes—it has been productive."[22]

At Burke's request, Leverton quietly monitored Congress to detect further efforts to "reform" the Defense Department and the services. Burke continued his letter-writing campaign. That October (1959), he expressed his views on defense organization to retired Vice Admiral Walter G. Schindler, explaining his opposition to unifying the services:

NH 55871

President Dwight D. Eisenhower, Secretary of the Navy Thomas S. Gates, Jr., and Admiral Arleigh A. Burke, Chief of Naval Operations, on board aircraft carrier *Saratoga* (CVA-60), June 1957.

> [O]ur present organization is . . . much better than a single Service for getting answers that are really thought through, for controlling the power contests among the many contending interests, for broadening and deepening the rigid Service concepts that would put us at the mercy of a flexible enemy. . . . A single Service would give effective control of the power of over $40 billion-plus a year into the hands of a single man, or a group of disciplined men all oriented in exactly the same direction, and this power would directly threaten the government of the country.[23]

It is important to note that Burke considered these points "basic and decisive," because what he did later appeared to violate the line dividing military and civilian authority.

In June 1960 Burke set up the Technical Studies Group (OP-06D) "to study the organization of the Department of Defense and to prepare studies . . . which the Secretary of the Navy and the Chief of Naval Operations could use in the event their views were sought by Congress or the executive branch of government."[24] The group, headed by Rear Admiral Denys W. Knoll, was created because "five bills had been introduced in the 86th Congress, 2nd session, which proposed substantial modification of the National Security Act of 1947 (Amended)."[25] Burke believed that the legislative furor was caused by an Air University study of defense organization and by an Air Force "Black Book" written for senior officers by the Air Staff. OP-06D thought that the Air Force intended to make one final push for service unification, but with proposals unlike those of 1947 or 1949. Instead, the Secretary of Defense would set the stage for unification with administrative changes, only asking for congressional approval after merger of the services was largely fact.[26] It was one reason why Burke strongly opposed creating the Joint Strategic Target Planning Staff—he viewed it as part of a proposal package, the end result of which would be Air Force domination of the military services.

Burke ordered Knoll to send weekly papers and letters to journalists sympathetic to the Navy's cause and Navy-oriented material to major public relations groups, expressing forcefully "what the Navy stands for and what the Navy will do."[27] Knoll also corresponded with many reserve and retired Navy personnel throughout the nation, asking them to "follow closely the public utterances of political candidates for national office and leading citizens in your area, and forward (direct to OP-06D as expeditiously as possible) a brief on what they are saying." As Knoll put it, his correspondents could "provide us in Washington with timely information concerning what we might expect when the New Congress convenes in January."[28] Not all recipients of this plea agreed that it was the proper procedure for the Navy Department to follow. One letter, which Knoll preserved, came back sharp: "Are we . . . to become Gallup Pollers to give strength of statistics to lobbying representatives of the Navy in the congressional corridors? This would seem to be a gross misuse of the men and funds appropriated to the Navy by that same Congress. I will not use the Navy mails to send this sort of information to you unless you reply with some justification I have not foreseen."[29] Knoll did not have a good answer to this complaint. He could not. He was fighting fire with fire.

Burke and Knoll had reason to be concerned. The political party platforms of both presidential candidates in 1960 called for more efficient defense organization, and the Democrats at their convention supported wholesale changes. In September 1960 John F. Kennedy, the Democratic nominee, chose Senator Stuart Symington (former Air Force Secretary during the unification hearings) to head a committee on defense reorganization. In response, Burke ordered the Navy's Judge Advocate General (JAG) to draft a response to what Burke thought the Symington Committee might produce. In October the JAG study, "Reorganization of the Department of Defense: Philosophy and Counter-Philosophy," was circulated in OPNAV. The JAG's position was that "any tendency to resist fundamental reorganization through attacks on the Air Force or response to the 'sinister conspiracy' theory not only misconstrues the basic issues, but may well bring about the very results which we seek to avoid."[30] The key issue was the relationship between "organizational problems" and "strategic problems. They cannot and must not be separated at any point."[31] Therefore, the Air Force favored unification, according to the JAG study, because of its approach to strategic warfare. Because the Navy considered that approach erroneous, the

Navy opposed unification—not because the Air Force favored unification.

In an October 1960 conference at the Pentagon, CNO Burke examined the JAG study. He criticized it for taking too long to make its important points and for containing "too much Air Force Phraseology."[32] In short, it was not partisan enough. The JAG responded that his study group had concluded that the only alternative to unification was "increasingly effective civilian control vested in the Secretary of Defense." Those at the conference took up the issue of the Navy's optimal strategy. Was the JAG's conclusion correct? The alternatives were as follows: (1) to increase the powers of some collective body instead of just those of the Secretary of Defense; (2) to go on the offensive against the Air Force by suggesting that the Tactical Air Command be given to the Army; (3) to give the Secretary of Defense more influence, but reduce the size of his office staff; and (4) to advocate a single chief of staff to counterbalance the powers of the Secretary of Defense. The conference rejected these alternatives. As the legal counsel to the Secretary of the Navy pointed out, "The Navy's greatest concern right now is to prevent another major DOD reorganization, or at least postpone it, for the Navy's position is stronger now than it has been for years and getting stronger all the time."[33]

Burke was not happy with a delaying strategy; that was not his style. The Navy was let off the hook, however, when the Symington Committee reported to the President-elect that December. The committee recommended eliminating the military departments and service secretaries, replacing the Assistant Secretaries of Defense with two powerful under secretaries, one each for weapons and administration, and substituting a single chief of staff for the JCS.[34] The report was seen as so extreme that it was largely ignored, and efforts in Congress to promote changes in defense administration fizzled. But CNO Burke well understood that the Secretary of Defense already had enough authority to reshape the Defense Department. The question was whether the next secretary would do it.

Burke's tenure as CNO lasted six years. When he was appointed CNO in 1955, OPNAV had just begun long-range force planning. Burke gave more influence to that planning process by linking it to Navy programming, the procedure by which operational requirements for new systems were translated into development goals for the Navy's bureaus. By linking programming to long-range planning and by giving OPNAV planning responsibility, Burke kept the leadership of Navy force development in OPNAV, which he dominated. The increased influence of planning should not have surprised anyone. The producer/consumer distinction was really a product of the war, when production and

710501 U.S. Navy
Secretary of the Navy William B. Franke, on the occasion of Admiral Arleigh Burke's swearing-in for a third term as Chief of Naval Operations, 17 August 1959.

consumption were in fact the major jobs of the bureaus, led by the Under Secretary of the Navy, and OPNAV. After the war, however, the Navy's needs changed. Systematic long-range force planning became the only way the Navy could anticipate technological and strategic changes and respond effectively to such changes. The cost of weapons and sensors grew more expensive in the 1950s, and getting ships and planes from the design stage to actual delivery in the fleet took longer. The relative scarcity of funds, time, and even personnel made long-range planning essential.

One very real problem with long-range planning was that it was a potentially powerful process. Consequently, questions such as, Who will the planners be? or Which OPNAV office will plan? or How will plans be converted into specific programs? were contentious. For that reason CNOs Carney and Burke placed their long-range planners in OP–93 (Long Range Objectives Group) close to the CNO. The proximity to Burke meant that planners had greater visibility at the highest levels. Eventually, long-range force level planning rivaled, then superseded, war planning as a place for younger flag officers to make names for themselves.[35] It is also important to remember that long-range planning could not be done effectively in a vacuum, isolated from the operations-oriented parts of OPNAV. The deputy chiefs acted as the key links to the bureaus and to the fleet. No planner who thought in terms of programs could ignore them. Indeed, turning plans into programs was impossible without including them in the process. But including the deputy chiefs made the program side of planning a consultative, pluralistic, interactive process—more a matter of coordination than direction, more a political process than one of command. The necessary emphasis on long-range planning gave the CNO an opportunity to lead the programming process. Whether he did or not was his choice, dependent on his skills.

By the end of Burke's third term (summer 1961), the program planning process within OPNAV was fairly comprehensive. The Director of the Long Range Objectives Group was responsible for projecting Navy missions and force requirements for ten to fifteen years. Guidance for OP-93 emanated from the CNO Advisory Board, whose membership included the Vice Chief of Naval Operations (chair), the director of OP-93, the deputy chiefs, the Assistant Commandant of the Marine Corps, the head of the Office of Naval Material, the Assistant Chief of Naval Operations for General Planning (OP-90), and the Director of Naval Administration (an assistant chief). As "the most influential body in the military requirements determinations and programming cycle," the advisory board evaluated "strategic concepts, research requirements and material and logistic readiness requirements."[36]

Directed by the CNO Advisory Board, OP-93 produced two plans: Long Range Requirements, for the next 10–15 years and Long Range Objectives, reasonable goals for fulfilling the requirements. The next step in the process rested with the ACNO for General Planning. Working from the Long Range Objectives, his office drew up guidelines for the deputy chiefs to follow as they put together their program objectives for the next fiscal year and for the nine years thereafter. Another Burke creation, the Program Evaluation Center, tracked the progress of the deputy chiefs and conducted "analyses of approved naval objectives; analysis, measurement of progress and display of approved programs of the Department of the Navy and evaluations of the impact of decisions and alternatives on program requirements."[37]

In the next step of program planning, DCNO planning staffs developed operational requirements based on the guidelines prepared by OP-90. Planning directorates and sometimes operations analysis groups of OP-01 (Personnel), OP-03 (Fleet Operations), OP-04 (Logistics), OP-05 (Air), and OP-07 (Development) worked with the Program Evaluation Center in OP-90. The deputy chiefs proceeded collectively from general force requirements, projected by OP-93, and fiscally constrained objectives, developed by OP-93, to program objectives, with performance milestones attached, prepared by DCNO offices. They forwarded their milestone requirements to the bureaus, where line managers entered detailed cost figures for each requirement. The link between the deputy chiefs and the bureaus was a group of officers called "program coordinators"— Navy captains and commanders who ensured that the detailed plans drawn up by the bureaus remained faithful to the program objectives worked out by the DCNO offices.[38]

The Navy's civilian leadership participated in the program planning process in several ways. First, the Secretary of the Navy chaired a top-level policy council, whose members included the under secretary, the CNO, the vice chief and the Marine Corps commandant. This group met at least every week to review Navy plans and policies. Second, the secretary used his Office of Analysis and Review to monitor Navy programs. Third, the comptroller reported Navy expenditures directly to the secretary, so the secretary could monitor the consequences of Navy program actions. Finally, the Program Evaluation Center in OP-90 reported simultaneously to the Navy secretary, the CNO, and the Marine Corps commandant.[39] The secretary's office was also the Navy's link to Congress. The assistant secretaries reported to Congress via the secretary in areas such as manpower, financial management, research and development, and procurement. Except through the CNO, however, the Secretary of the Navy did not participate in major Navy force structure decisions.

Burke developed the organization of program planning over time. The first Long Range Requirements document, for example, was not produced until April 1960. It took time because Burke had to reconcile his command philosophy, which emphasized decentralization, with a program planning system that was centralized. Burke described his approach to command as "management at the lowest possible competent level . . . [s]o that, in the ideal situation, with . . . competent people and experience up and down the line, the top of the organization makes policy decisions, only."[40] That philosophy was consistent with his experience as a line officer and a bureau (Ordnance) manager. But the need to do serious program planning, coupled with the need to do battle with the proponents of unification and those hostile to the Navy's strategic role, forced Burke to shape OPNAV more like a *personal* staff— in short, to do what Burke criticized the Army and Air Force for already having done. The centralization of the Army staff system insinuated itself upon OPNAV, despite Burke's efforts to keep the programming activity open to ideas from officers fresh from the fleet. For example, he classified both the Long Range Requirements and the Long Range Objectives no higher than Secret, so that OPNAV's junior officers could see and comment on them.

Burke was able to make OPNAV a staff, yet keep it Navy, because of his own fierce dedication and hard work. Rosenberg quoted Burke's comments on fatigue: ". . . you get very tired. It takes a lot of stamina for that job. You work seven days a week and you're lucky if you can get seven hours sleep a night."[41] In OPNAV, Burke's energy and time were spent leading and pushing the program planning process that he had devised. As the Assistant Secretary of Defense (Comptroller) noted in November 1961, "the making of critical decisions in the Navy (e.g., force structure) involves the collective participation of the entire CNO organization." The comptroller also observed that the CNO and the Secretary of the Navy more often *approved* than *decided*: "The real decision–making occurs during the collective process of staffing, review, approval, and agreement as the development of the planning document proceeds from stage to stage."[42] The danger of such a system was apparent to Burke: officers outside senior leadership positions could in fact influence major decisions without bearing a commensurate share of responsibility for those decisions. But that was a danger unavoidable in any complex organization. The benefit of such a system was that it tapped the multiple sources of expertise within the organization.

KE 70427 U.S. Air Force

The Pentagon, headquarters and symbol of the U.S. Defense Establishment.

5

The McNamara Revolution

When President Kennedy appointed Robert McNamara Secretary of Defense in 1961, he instructed him to increase the effectiveness of the nation's armed forces without taking a larger share of the budget. At the same time Congress was waiting to see how McNamara would use the authority granted his office by the 1958 DOD Reorganization Act. McNamara was under pressure from both the President and the Congress to create a stronger, more effective military force *and* economize on the defense budget. McNamara thought he could do both simultaneously, and as part of his effort to achieve these goals, he instituted the Planning, Programming, and Budgeting System (PPBS).

PPBS was a major shock for the services, but not because it brought the concept of programming to military administration. The shock came from McNamara's claim that his office could and would set programs, monitor the services in meeting program goals, and, if necessary, enforce service compliance with the secretary's policies. The Office of the Secretary of Defense put into place standard operating procedures that gave OSD both the initiative and the power of review in the programming and budgeting process. In effect, this management system allowed McNamara and his deputies to control the structure and the routines of organizations like OPNAV. According to Rosenberg, "Burke felt that he was never able to find out just what it was that McNamara believed in or wanted to accomplish as Secretary of Defense."[1] Was it any wonder? What Burke and his colleagues had created McNamara would have to dominate or destroy.

The memory of McNamara's management style is fading now, but his ideas, attitudes, and methods colored every aspect of defense decision making during the years he was Defense secretary. Indeed, McNamara was so convinced that his concepts and procedures of defense management were correct that he deliberately kept forceful personalities out of service chief and service secretary positions, and he moved ruthlessly against those military officers who criticized his authority. In the Navy's case, historian Paul Schratz observed: "McNamara also wished to prevent the naval leadership from undercutting his authority via a traditional end run to a sympathetic naval ear in the White House. The naval secretary's chair, therefore, required . . . the least enthusiastic Kennedy supporter in government."[2] That meant the man who had managed Senator Lyndon Johnson's campaign for the Democratic Party's presidential nomination in 1960, John B. Connally,

Jr. Burke's successor as Chief of Naval Operations was Admiral George W. Anderson, Jr., an aviator with extensive command and joint staff experience. He barely made it through one two-year term (1961–1963) as CNO because he angered the Secretary of Defense twice: first, privately, during the blockade of Cuba in October 1962; and then, publicly, in congressional testimony against McNamara's controversial proposal for a multiservice fighter plane, the TFX.[3]

In the early 1960s McNamara and his assistants believed the secretary had a mandate from the President, as well as being under pressure from Congress, to reform the Defense Department. They did not trust the uniformed leaders of the services, and they expected the Secretary of Defense to control military procurement and policy through the Planning, Programming, and Budgeting System.

In August 1961 McNamara ordered Charles Hitch, Assistant Secretary of Defense (Comptroller), to "develop a plan for a Department of Defense integrated system for relating programming, budgeting and financing, accounting, and progress and status reporting."[4] The Five Year Force Structure and Financial Program, later called the Five Year Defense Program, emerged from this effort. McNamara's goal was to give the Office of the Secretary of Defense the capacity (it already had the authority) to plan across service lines for a significant time period. To accomplish that, McNamara and his deputies first divided all the missions performed by the services into a set of generic programs such as "strategic warfare" and "conventional warfare." Then they created a system for expressing the costs of those programs in terms such as personnel, operations and maintenance, and research and development, which Congress used in the appropriations process. As Hitch testified before Congress, "the functional arrangement of the budget [i.e., the one used by Congress] . . . does not focus on forces and military programs in relation to missions, the key decision-making area of principal concern to top management in the Defense Department."[5]

To solve the problem, which Hitch described, PPBS gave Congress and the Office of the Secretary of Defense the same basic data but in two different forms. For Congress, expenditures were listed by basic functional categories such as operations and maintenance, research and development, and ship construction (for the Navy). Within OSD, the same information was organized by program categories such as nuclear strategic forces, general purpose forces, and command, control, and communications systems. Before McNamara instituted PPBS, the military services had their own ways of planning and tracking expenditures, based usually on force level projections. The Navy, for example, projected what ships and aircraft it would need to perform its missions and then decided what those forces would cost in terms of funds and personnel. Under PPBS, the services translated their force projections into the program categories created by OSD and then projected the spending figures five years. OSD used this information to evaluate service trends as well as immediate spending requests.

The Secretary of Defense wanted to compare the cost-effectiveness of various programs that performed, in his view, the same mission. For example, what was the more cost-effective means of insuring that a surprise nuclear attack by the Soviet Union did not destroy the ability of the United States to retaliate successfully—build more Polaris missiles and launching submarines, or buy more Minuteman missiles for hardened, land-based silos? By comparing total systems, considered the basic building blocks of major defense programs, OSD could determine which service recommendations to accept. McNamara's system provided Congress with budget figures in functional categories including personnel, operations, support, procurement, while it let the secretary compare and evaluate service proposals in program categories.

What linked data from program categories with that from functional categories was the process of budgeting Total Obligational Authority, defined as "the full cost of an annual increment of a program regardless of the year in which the funds [were] authorized, appropriated, or expended."[6] By dividing each major program, such as strategic forces, into basic elements, such as the Polaris/SSBN combination, McNamara and Hitch could determine how much that element should cost in terms of personnel, operations and maintenance, and procurement. They could also decide how much each element contributed to the overall program (strategic forces, or nuclear deterrence) over a five-year period. Under Burke, program planning in OPNAV had not been directly linked to the budgeting process because the budget categories did not coincide with program categories, which were stated in terms of force structure. Navy leaders had to accept PPBS despite the fact that it displaced their own methods of programming, but they most strongly objected to the secretary's use of cost-effectiveness studies, conducted by his own Directorate of Systems Analysis, in determining which service systems were approved by the secretary for the overall defense budget sent to Congress.

Secretary Connally's replacement (Connally had resigned to run for governor of Texas), Fred H. Korth, responded to the changes emanating from McNamara's office by appointing John S. Dillon, a career assistant to Navy secretaries since 1947, chairman of a board of inquiry. Composed of uniformed and civilian officials drawn from the Navy Department, the Dillon Board examined internal Navy management and policymaking and external influences that affected Navy decisions. In six months of study (June through November 1962),

Secretary of the Navy Fred H. Korth (*right*) and administrative assistant
John H. Dillon tour Pearl Harbor, 1963.

the Dillon Board reviewed the management of the Navy Department and
specifically recommended changes that would foster a more effective
organization for OPNAV and the Navy Secretariat.

With regard to the Office of the Secretary of Defense, the Dillon Board's
External Environmental Influences Study took a long-standing Navy
position that the Secretary of Defense was encroaching on service
prerogatives. However, the "consolidation of decision making is being
accomplished not by the reorganization of existing components but by
requiring the presentation of detailed information so that it can be
evaluated and acted upon at top levels."[7] The Dillon Board viewed
programming as "the primary tool of both financial management and
military management."[8] Expressed another way, "the management
information system must be designed to account not only for the
traditional documents of obligation and expenditure, but must consider
many other events that provide controls over the physical aspects of the
projected military structure."[9] In short, McNamara was indeed taking
over.

The Dillon Board concluded that the Navy would have to change its
internal management to respond to McNamara's aggressive use of
program budgeting and analysis. However, the services were not the

only institutions that felt threatened by the new budget process. The armed services and appropriations committees of Congress also feared that PPBS was reducing their control over defense policy and expenditures. The appropriations committees believed that the traditional congressional budget categories (e.g., operations and maintenance, research and development), were no longer adequate to give Congress real control over military force structure. The armed services committees, on the other hand, feared that their traditional control over force structure and composition was being transferred to appropriations committees because of PPBS. Accordingly, the armed services committees required the services to get their permission annually to purchase aircraft, missiles, or ships. Concerned that McNamara had taken complete control over defense planning, Congress retaliated by ignoring McNamara and demanding information from the military services. As the Dillon Board recognized, the need to give both OSD *and* Congress the data they demanded placed a new burden on OPNAV.

According to a Dillon study, the Navy found it difficult to respond to OSD and congressional pressures because the Navy was not well enough organized internally. The board's *Planning, Programming, Budget, and Appraising Study* reported that "all bureaus have established their own internal programs, which in most cases do not coincide with programs identified in the OSD program system or the OPNAV system. Bureau programs are generally more closely associated to the appropriation structure than to the OSD program structure."[10] Put another way, the bureaus were still oriented toward Congress. Moreover, the Assistant Chief of Naval Operations for General Planning and Programming (OP-90) "does not have direction authority for the over-all programming process with respect to major Departmental components, or within the Office of the Chief of Naval Operations."[11] Yet OP-90 was responsible for submitting the Navy's programming data to the Office of the Secretary of Defense. If OSD held the Navy accountable to the program choices made by the Secretary of Defense, then the Navy's civilian and military leaders would have to create a programming office with more authority to meet OSD's demands. McNamara was forcing versions of his management institutions on the services.

Former Secretary of the Navy Forrestal once claimed that the Navy was administered by "mutual consent": "The bureaus have legal existence; they enjoy a mutual independence; they have . . . concrete, well-defined jobs to do. . . . They have also information and they have money. In other words they possess everything which gives purpose, logic, and meaning to action."[12] Burke had acted to reduce bureau independence; McNamara was reducing it further. But technology had already made the bureau system obsolete. As officials in the Bureau of Ships reported, the relationship between a modern ship's hull and machinery, on the one hand, and its weapons and sensors, on the other, was becoming so intimate and complex that "there is in many cases . . . a complete intermesh of [bureau] responsibilities and in fact no clear responsibility or authority."[13] The Dillon Board understood the cost of maintaining bureau autonomy: "Of the nine DLG's under construction in a recent month, six were behind schedule an average of 6 months each. The estimated additional cost . . . is $200,000 per month per ship. A substantial portion of this added cost may be attributed to incompatibility of companion equipments developed by [the Bureau of Ships and the Bureau of Naval Weapons]."[14]

To deal with the administrative challenge posed by new technology, the Dillon Board proposed that OPNAV reorganize its program sponsorship. "For example, the Deputy Chief of Naval Operations (Air) is the appropriation sponsor for the Procurement of Aircraft and Missiles Appropriation, which includes among other things surface-to-air missiles. The latter are the *programming* responsibility of the Deputy Chief of Naval Operations (Fleet Operations and Readiness)."[15] In short, the board proposed that program sponsors serve also as appropriation sponsors, so that the same OPNAV office would defend its work in both Congress and OSD.

The long and detailed Dillon Report in fact contained inconsistencies. The report accepted the Navy's traditional approach to the distribution of authority within the department, recommending that the bureaus continue to function and that the Secretary of the Navy oversee logistics. At the same time the board argued that the "lead bureau" system of management, originally proposed by the Libby Board in 1956, was not giving the Navy the advanced systems it needed at a cost it could afford. The board also found some assignments of responsibility "ambiguous," particularly in the bureaus of Naval Material (created to coordinate the actions of the other bureaus) and Supplies and Accounts (nominally subordinate to the Chief of Naval Material). The responsibilities of these chiefs overlapped so much that "neither knows exactly when his responsibilities begin and end."[16] Faced with closer congressional scrutiny and a determined, able Defense secretary, the board temporized, unwilling to recommend major changes.

To improve coordination among programs, the Dillon Board wanted the Secretary of the Navy to appoint a chief of naval support as the Navy's "producer executive." Although the board accepted the traditional distinction between producers and consumers, it believed that an office *above* the bureaus could pull together the different threads of Navy development and production. While the board accepted the distinction between OPNAV as consumer and the bureaus as producers, it reaffirmed the Navy secretary's control over "logistics administration." In a strongly worded dissent to the report, Admiral Claude V. Ricketts, Vice Chief of Naval Operations, asserted that the proposed chief of naval support would never be effective because the Dillon Board had refused to recommend giving the position the resources to function effectively as a new office.[17]

Ricketts was on the right track. The Dillon Report reaffirmed the Navy's traditional bilinear administration at the same time it cited examples of confusion caused by decentralized administration. One of the major points in the report, for example, criticized the fragmented responsibility for managing shore activities.[18] Yet the board did not recommend that one office in the Navy be given sole responsibility in that area. Similar criticism was leveled against "double-hatting" the jobs of Deputy Chief of Naval Operations for Personnel and Naval Reserve (OP-01) and Chief of Naval Personnel. The two positions had been combined so that the bureau director could better advise the CNO on staffing, recruiting, and training. But the combination was not working. As Admiral Charles K. Duncan, who later held both positions, observed, "I consider the position of Chief of Naval Personnel with its concurrent position of Deputy Chief of Naval Operations for Manpower and Reserve, to be such a complex one and such a demanding one that it is in a sense almost beyond the capabilities of any one person to do what I would term a perfect job."[19] The Dillon Report suggested separating the positions again, especially because the Secretary of Defense was demanding explicit justification of the Navy's billet structure. As the board admitted, the CNO had to "assume the full responsibility to determine both the qualitative and quantitative requirements for military manpower."[20] The dilemma remained: there was no obvious way to separate the positions and still work out their respective spheres of authority.

Yet some means had to be found to administer a personnel and training system capable of producing the skilled people required to operate all the new systems entering the fleet. Unlike the 1950s, younger officers now actually feared that postgraduate work in technical fields would "endanger their opportunities for promotion," especially if a system they trained in became obsolescent. The Dillon Report showed that "current personnel practices tend to substantiate that view. The truth is that the Navy has not yet worked out a logical career pattern of technical subspecialization."[21] The shortage of technically trained officers meant that OPNAV could not provide the essential requirements for new weapons systems. It also meant that bureaus would lack talented commanders. Senior Navy officers, including former CNO Burke, had insisted that the structure of an organization counted for less than the quality of its people. In that sense, the Navy was going downhill. As the board admitted: "The view that tours of duty in key technical positions in bureaus and shore activities adversely affect promotional opportunities to flag rank is widely held among officers. These problems are most serious."[22] The Dillon Board had avoided saying that the Navy, with its emphasis on operations and on decentralized authority and administration, had backed itself into a corner. The pressures from the Office of the Secretary of Defense only made more apparent the costs of preserving a very loose staff in OPNAV and semiautonomous bureaus. Given the new and growing influence of the Secretary of Defense and OSD, the Navy had to reform its own administration.

The Dillon Report is a detailed snapshot of the Navy's administration in 1962. Although the study presented an excellent diagnosis of the Navy's administrative problems, it failed to dig deep enough. Was the bureau system outmoded? If so, what should replace it? Could an organization as splintered as OPNAV defend itself against the new Secretary of Defense? If so, how? Should OPNAV be organized along functional lines, such as personnel, operations, and logistics, or should the major deputies to the CNO represent the major Navy platform communities (submarines, surface ships, and planes)? These questions would surface later in another study.

In the meantime, the Secretary of Defense was undoubtedly pleased that such issues had not become the focus of an open and ongoing dialogue among senior Navy officers. McNamara had not consulted with the services in 1961 before he imposed a set of rules and procedures (PPBS) that allowed OSD to drive service program planning. And, once PPBS was in place, he avoided naming service secretaries who might challenge its suitability. "McNamara saw a strong, analytical type of service secretary" could become a "rallying point for service loyalties" and "hence a divisive threat to his own exercise of authority."[23] The secretary's actions were aimed at preventing the services from challenging his control. For example, McNamara chose not to release the original studies of the Defense Department, undertaken right after the Kennedy administration entered the White House.[24] Moreover, the continuous administrative changes emanating from McNamara's office kept the services off balance. As Assistant Secretary of Defense for Administration Sol Horwitz said in an interview: "Not only is the Defense structure highly dynamic, it is safe to say that it will continue to be highly dynamic. . . . A static condition would be a certain sign of management stagnation."[25] Although a faith in reorganization was a tenet of modern management, the process of redistributing responsibility and authority was (and remains) a tool for keeping the opposition from coalescing.

Certain officers in OPNAV viewed the new Defense secretary and his assistants as far more dangerous than the advocates of unification in the 1940s. To these officers, McNamara and his colleagues were cloaking a campaign to suffocate "the military profession . . . as an authoritative voice" in the guise of promoting efficiency.[26] An OP-06 (Plans and Policy) study put it this way: "there is every evidence that every function performed by the Military Department Secretaries, other than problems of military strategy, the management of military forces, and the related development of weapons systems, will come under the immediate policy control of some functionary or activity in the Office of the Secretary of Defense."[27] This development threatened the Navy's line officers who needed a leader "to stand up for the operating forces and the men who operated them in the everlasting battle to protect their (and the Nation's) interests against unduly restrictive administrative procedures in the name of economy and the democratic ethic."[28] How had John Paul Jones phrased it in his letter to the Continental Congress? "A navy is essentially and necessarily aristocratic."

But this "aristocracy" was not based on privilege, nor in the modern Navy did it govern arbitrarily. Command in the Navy can best be expressed by two accepted maxims: (1) "No question should ever be decided without considering *primarily* its effect on the efficiency of the fleet for *war*," and (2) "Avoid hostile criticism of authority."[29] The emphasis is always on operations and the chain of command. Operations will succeed only if "proper" leadership is based on a clear understanding of the problem at hand, of the abilities of the men ordered to solve it, and of the risks involved. The old Navy tradition was that men, properly led and organized, could do almost anything. But that tradition assumed that "good" leaders would focus on the *real* problem—what would bring victory in war. It also assumed that Navy officers governed, instead of ruled, the men entrusted to them. That is, officers established their legitimacy through their own performance— leading instead of coercing. The chain of command was in fact a chain of obligations—seniors supporting subordinates and subordinates accepting the authority of seniors. The chain of command was not primarily an organizational structure, but was, and still is, basically an ethical bond, linking warriors as commanders and commanded in settings where no other kind of link—especially that found in bureaucracies—will work.

Since the end of the Second World War, OPNAV has had problems linking the concepts of management and leadership as understood by Navy line officers. That had been easy when the CNO was both manager and operational leader. Indeed, a CNO's influence often varied with his image as a strong operator. Through operations, a CNO like Burke, for example, could affirm and strengthen his authority within the Navy. When the CNO lost operational command authority, he and his office lost much of their legitimacy. When Secretary of Defense McNamara increased the authority of OSD at the expense of the service headquarters, he further undermined the stature and authority of the Chief of Naval Operations. In addition, he attacked the twin pillars of Navy command tradition—the chain of command and the emphasis on operations. If, as seemed true, the CNO was just a bureaucratic subordinate to a Navy secretary who, in turn, was a subordinate to a dominant Defense secretary, then the Navy's chain of command led ultimately to an official who was not necessarily experienced in command. And if systems analysts could make decisions that were once made by officers with years of operational command experience, then it would seem that operations were no longer considered a source of legitimacy for naval officers. But, of course, operations mattered because the legitimacy of officers in the fleet—the right to command—would crumble if they did not.

McNamara could not understand the intimate connection between legitimacy and operations. His concept of authority worked well in business areas but inadequately in military institutions. For example, in May 1965 the secretary directed the services to apply the project manager concept to major development efforts.[30] The project manager held the power and the responsibility to push through a major project, like the Polaris submarine, from design to delivery. So long as this manager and his subordinates met production and testing deadlines agreed upon with OSD, they were guaranteed support. The project manager concept undermined the programming authority of OPNAV and sent a signal to the bureaus that they were seen as obstacles to effective technological development. McNamara interpreted the management and coordination problems in OPNAV and between OPNAV and the bureaus, which were highlighted in the 1962 Dillon Report, as evidence of a poorly organized and managed Navy. Conversely, senior Navy officers viewed the problem of interbureau coordination as a price they had to pay for the Navy's bilinear, decentralized administration. These uniformed leaders failed to make McNamara understand that the Navy's shared, decentralized, and often confusing administration was something worth preserving and vital to the Navy's concept of command authority.

From one perspective, however, Secretary McNamara was correct. The Navy's bilinear organization made sense when the Secretary of the Navy was the senior civilian in the Navy Department, ensuring civilian control, and when the CNO held the operational authority. But after 1958, the Office of the Secretary of Defense replaced the service secretaries as the agency of civilian control, while the commanders in

1096797-B U.S. Navy

With Secretary of the Navy Paul H. Nitze at his side, Secretary of Defense Robert S. McNamara addresses the media at the naval shipyard in Portsmouth, New Hampshire, April 1964.

chief displaced the service chiefs in the chains of command. Because the CINCs did not in fact command their component commanders the way the CNO had commanded the Navy before the 1958 law passed, the CNO had to contend with other senior officers, such as the Commander in Chief, Pacific, for the image of senior Navy commander. Moreover, the need for administratively separate bureaus reporting to the Secretary of the Navy no longer existed. Instead, the real need was for responsiveness to the Office of the Secretary of Defense. As CNO David L. McDonald discovered to his disappointment, the duty to OSD increased his "managerial and administrative responsibilities" while "the number of his command prerogatives shrank."[31]

Supported by Secretary of the Navy Paul H. Nitze (McNamara's former Assistant Secretary of Defense for International Security Affairs), McNamara asked Congress in 1966 to eliminate the Navy's material bureaus and to allow the Secretary of the Navy to subordinate them to the CNO through the Chief of Naval Material.[32] Secretary Nitze shared McNamara's belief that the Navy needed reorganizing. As one of "McNamara's men," Nitze came to his post committed to bringing the Navy in line with what he and McNamara considered modern organizational practices.[33] The new Navy secretary ordered the Navy's Chief of Information to draw up a public affairs plan for the new department.[34] Nitze also had Admiral McDonald establish a Systems

Analysis Division (OP–96) in OPNAV, so that the CNO could better respond to the information and analysis requirements that OSD was forcing on the military headquarters staffs.

In 1963 then-Secretary of the Navy Fred Korth had responded to the Dillon Board recommendations by requiring the material bureaus (Weapons, Ships, and Yards and Docks) to report to him through the Chief of Naval Material. General Order Number 5 was altered in July 1963 to reflect the new relationships, and the Chief of Naval Material formally became the head of what was called the Naval Material Support Establishment. But two years later Secretary Nitze expanded the order to clarify the role of the Chief of Naval Material. He asked Admiral Ignatius J. Gallantin, the new chief, to consider changes and additions to the Naval Material Support Establishment. By 1966 Nitze had a proposal for McNamara, which the latter submitted to the congressional armed services committees.

In a March 1966 letter to the Chairman of the House Armed Services Committee, he noted, "The Secretary of the Navy believes that the organizations performing the Navy's material support functions should be so structured as to subject them to more effective command by the Chief of Naval Material under the Chief of Naval Operations."[35] Congress abolished the statutory basis of the bureaus and gave the Secretary of the Navy the responsibility (once the prerogative of Congress) for assigning the bureau organizations their functions. McNamara also described what the altered organization would look like: "the Naval Material Command will be divided along functional lines into six subcommands—namely, the Air Systems Command, the Ship Systems Command, the Ordnance Systems Command, the Electronic Systems Command, the Supply Systems Command, and the Facilities Engineering Command, each under a commander."[36] The bureaus of Medicine and Personnel were also placed under the Chief of Naval Operations. The traditional consumer/ producer distinction was dropped, and the CNO became responsible for all naval support elements that had once reported to the secretary through the Naval Material Support Establishment.

To make the transition from the bureaus to the newly formed systems commands a smoother one, Admiral Gallantin and the Assistant Chief of Naval Operations for Program Planning (OP–090) analyzed the functions of the new commands and their relationships to OPNAV during April and May 1966.[37] The transition from bureaus to systems commands took over four months to implement and was complete by August 1966. It was achieved only through lengthy negotiations over the respective powers of OPNAV and the Naval Material Command because former bureau personnel, accustomed to a certain level of autonomy, had

711075 U.S. Navy

Vice Admiral David L. McDonald (*left*), Commander Sixth Fleet, discusses fleet operations with Admiral George W. Anderson, Chief of Naval Operations, May 1962. The following year McDonald succeeded Anderson as CNO.

feared that their independence would dissipate in the systems commands.[38]

An in-depth study of OPNAV, supervised by Rear Admiral Roy S. Benson, Assistant Vice Chief of Naval Operations, paralleled the transition to systems commands.[39] Prodded by McNamara's defense "reforms," OPNAV had changed by fits and starts under CNOs Anderson and McDonald. The Benson Task Force reviewed those changes and devised a reorganization plan to prepare the office for its new role of directing systems commands in a setting where OSD dominated service program planning. To hold down the size of OPNAV, the task force recommended that the Chief of Naval Operations create intelligence and communication commands separate from OPNAV. The ACNO positions for Communications (OP–94) and Intelligence (OP–92) could be "double-hatted," serving simultaneously as members of the CNO's staff and as directors of their own commands.[40] The task force was compelled to recommend this organizational gimmick because supervising the systems commands would impose new demands on OPNAV.

Benson and his colleagues formally completed their study of OPNAV organization at the end of 1966. They observed the following:

• OPNAV's organization and working procedures have not been reoriented to conform to the 1 May 1966 reorganization of the Navy Department.

- The basic organization of OPNAV is not responsive to some of the demands placed upon it and is unwieldy in operation. . . .

- [T]he OP-090 [Program Planning] organization is a layer between the DCNO's and the VCNO, slowing down the processing of paperwork and preventing the DCNO's from exercising a level of authority which would relieve more senior officers of some of the burden placed upon them.

- OPNAV personnel are involved too deeply in the details of functions performed by subordinate commands. . . .

- The span of control of the VCNO and certain other officials in OPNAV is excessive.

- A common complaint of certain DCNO's is that so many of their personnel are involved in studies that it detracts to a degree from their ability to carry out their primary duties.[41]

- [OPNAV program sponsors dealt directly with project managers in the systems commands without going through the new Naval Material Command.][42]

These findings suggest that the problems plaguing OPNAV in 1966 were much like those afflicting OSD at the same time. That is, as McNamara forced his management form and style on the service headquarters, the problems of overcentralization, overwork, and continual appraisal and review grew more serious in his own office. The emphasis on programming as the key management tool caused most of the major problems. If programming were indeed the primary means by which the Defense secretary controlled the services, and if the CNO had to apply the same technique to control the Navy, then the Navy's tradition of decentralization and delegation would collapse. Under the new system, a conflict between the ACNO for Program Planning and the deputy chiefs was inevitable because the latter were authorized deputies of the CNO and the former only a staff assistant to the CNO. Who was actually in charge—the authorized deputies or the staff analysts? Similarly, the military had criticized McNamara for placing too much power, through PPBS, in the hands of an OSD staff responsible only to the Secretary of Defense. The same critique applied to Program Planning and the newly created Systems Analysis Division. The Navy was developing what it was criticizing in OSD. (See Figure 3.)

Similarly, the CNO and the VCNO's work load had grown too great. Under the Program, Planning, and Budgeting System, neither dared allow authorized deputies to act independently. But the DCNO positions were originally created to shield the Chief and Vice Chief of

OFFICE OF THE CHIEF OF NAVAL OPERATIONS, 1966

Figure 3

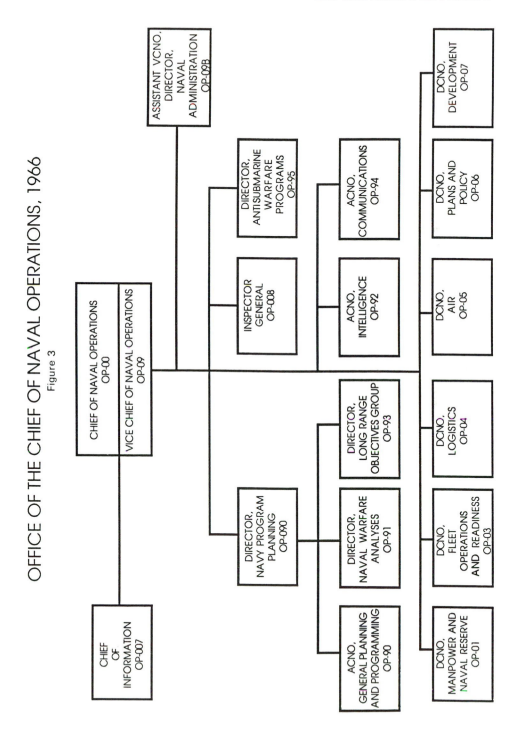

Naval Operations from work that was better delegated. The villain was McNamara's concept of programming. For programming to be an effective tool of organizational control, top management must monitor the program proposals, which lower layers (divisions) of the organization periodically prepare. In a large organization like the Defense Department, however, top managers have neither the time nor the energy to monitor all the program documentation, which the service staffs prepare. As a result, they use their own staff analysts to review proposals from the services, and influence over programming decisions devolves unavoidably to those analysts. To counter this influence, the service chiefs hire or train their own program analysts. The process repeats itself within each service as deputies of the service chief develop or hire their own analytical experts to shield their branches against the service chief's analysts. This process of using analysis as the primary decision tool creates friction between staff analysts and line deputies. This friction was unavoidable, however, because the CNO's perspective was strongly influenced by the studies done in OP-96 (Systems Analysis), which tried to anticipate the analyses performed at the OSD level. As McNamara realized, reviewing program elements only gave his office veto power. To stay ahead of the services—to push defense policy instead of just regulating it—he needed to conduct analyses independently of the services. Although the Navy opposed this policy, the CNO welcomed a staff analysis organization to justify his programs in terms that OSD would accept.

McNamara's approach to PPBS had a domino effect. The concept of systems analysis cascaded down the levels of the Navy's organization. Studies, once a luxury, became essential. As the CNO's deputies acquired analytic support, either directly from the Center for Naval Analyses, or indirectly from outside contractors (the so-called Beltway Bandits), a "shadow" OPNAV staff grew.

The emphasis on programming also had other side-effects: the bypassing of the chain of command and the reduction in the influence of OP-06 (Plans and Policy) as the CNO's role in the JCS was overshadowed by his programming responsibilities. Deputies of program sponsors (the DCNOs) dealt directly with project managers in the systems commands, often ignoring the offices in the Naval Material Command with official cognizance over programs. Officers in NAVMAT and in the systems commands found that OPNAV program directors, responsible to program sponsors, would go around them and deal directly with the managers of key projects. As Rear Admiral Benson pointed out to the OPNAV staff, its proper function was review and approval, "not day to day detailed monitoring." But that statement missed the point.[43] Programming was a form of control, and control was now

OPNAV's responsibility. The bilinear Navy was gone. The question was, What would take its place?

There was already one alternative in place, one structured around a weapons system. Vice Admiral Rickover had recreated in the Bureau of Ships (later Naval Ship Systems Command) an organization modeled after the old Bureau of Aeronautics. BUAER had been unique among the material bureaus before the Second World War because of its control over aviation personnel training and assignments. The first chief of BUAER had won and kept that power through nearly a decade of bureaucratic conflict with the Office of the Chief of Naval Operations and other bureaus, especially Navigation (later the Bureau of Personnel). BUAER was able to get away with its sweeping authority because its first chief argued persuasively that the Navy's fledgling air arm needed special protection and support.[44] By the mid-1960s Rickover, as an official in both the Atomic Energy Commission and in the Bureau of Ships, had used the same approach and the same rationale to gain control over the design and construction of nuclear submarines for the U.S. Navy, and over the training and assignment of the personnel to man those submarines. He had, through his contacts in Congress and through his post at the Atomic Energy Commission, created a bureau-within-a-bureau, gradually insulating himself from effective control by the CNO. Instead of responding to his OPNAV sponsor, Rickover controlled

Rear Admiral Hyman G. Rickover listens to a status report of the power plant on board the Navy's first nuclear-powered submarine, *Nautilus* (SSN-571).
1037271

the sponsor through his ties to Congress. As Rickover admitted, he was a "creature of Congress."[45] By the 1970s Rickover's influence was so great that it extended to submarine operations as well as design.

Rickover's story has been told in detail elsewhere.[46] What matters here is that his approach to weapons development and force planning was an alternative considered by the Benson Task Force. Although Rickover's tactics bypassed the chain of command, he had succeeded in creating, training, and supporting a large nuclear submarine force. Moreover, he was willing to accept other branches of the Navy. All he demanded was that, if they used nuclear power, the power plants be his designs manned by his crews. The task force avoided praising Rickover because the admiral had only reluctantly accepted OPNAV authority. Indeed, when Admiral Elmo R. Zumwalt, Jr., served as Chief of Naval Operations (1970-1974), he found that he had to negotiate with the nominally subordinate Rickover as an equal before drafting a ship construction program. What the task force did acknowledge, however, was that OPNAV could be restructured above and around "weapons systems directorates," or the reorganized systems commands. What the task force also understood, but did not say, was that such an organization might well head off future Rickovers in the bureaus.

After considering OPNAV's organizational possibilities for nine months, the Benson Task Force arrived at five basic structural alternatives:

1. The *"four forces"* structure with DCNOs for undersea warfare, surface warfare, air warfare, and mobile combat logistics support (or amphibious warfare); and two other DCNOs for strategic plans and policy, and programs and budget. The Chief of Naval Material would be subordinate to these deputy chiefs.

2. The *functional-processes* structure, with DCNOs for planning and programming, development, manpower, logistics, and fleet operations and readiness. Again, the Chief of Naval Material would be subordinate to the DCNOs.

3. The *weapons systems directorates*, with DCNOs for manpower, operations, logistics, plans, development, and programming/budgeting. Six special directorates—for ships, aviation, logistics, facilities, ordnance, and electronics—would replace the Naval Material Command. The head of each would report directly to the program sponsors in OPNAV.

4. The *sequential-processes* structure, with DCNOs for programming/budgeting, planning and policy analysis, execution and

appraisal, and "futures." Assistant chiefs of naval operations for antisubmarine warfare, aviation, research and development, electronic warfare, amphibious warfare, communications, and intelligence would head other OPNAV offices. These program directors would work directly with project managers in the systems commands, and the identity of each special office headed by an ACNO would change as naval warfare changed.

5. The *existing* structure, organized around both functional (e.g., planning,) and force (e.g., air, surface, ASW) concepts.[47]

The task force had been open to all the alternatives, but stressed that "one of the basic principles underlying our effort has been to assign functions at the lowest practicable level."[48] In a memo to the CNO Advisory Board in October 1966, Benson observed: "Implementation of the Four Forces concept . . . would not be difficult. We operate almost like that now." However, he also reminded the members of the advisory board that "a basic change in the structure of CNO's staff is not essential." Benson and his task force well knew of "the turmoil incident to change," and the changes in OPNAV forced by the Secretary of Defense had already taken enough time and energy to implement.[49] Although the task force was willing to accept OPNAV as it existed, it also reaffirmed the traditional commitment to delegation and decentralization.

The Benson study put some important issues on the table. OPNAV had been functionally organized after the Second World War, but by 1966 it was a hybrid headquarters organization built around forces and functions—part platform-oriented, part OSD-oriented (especially Program Planning), and part JCS-oriented (Plans and Policy). The 1966 reorganization had not really dealt with the effects of this patchwork structure, and the Benson study clearly stated that certain problems in the Navy were a consequence of it. The study also showed that influence within OPNAV was focused around the three major operational communities—aviators, submariners, and surface ship officers. The idea of organizing around these communities, however, was not new. In 1950, for example, Vice Admiral F. W. Low, the special advisor on undersea warfare to the CNO, argued in a classified but influential study that the "organization for Undersea Warfare should be . . . either under a specially appointed Deputy Chief of Naval Operations or as a fleet organization along the lines of the Tenth Fleet in World War II."[50] What was novel in 1966 was saying that such an organization could work.

The Dillon Board had stated this challenge to OPNAV in its 1962 report: "There is a compelling need for the establishment of a doctrine around which our executives and the organizations which they supervise can better coordinate their collective efforts." This doctrine was "essential to achievement of the discipline necessary for unity in their leadership."[51] But what doctrine? The "four forces" form of organization called for multiple doctrines. No one doctrine would meld all the pieces of OPNAV together. Rear Admiral Benson tried to build a consensus among senior flag officers behind *some* doctrine in 1967, but CNO McDonald left office that year, handing over his position to Admiral Thomas H. Moorer. When Moorer came in, the search for a consensus had to begin all over again. This is not to say that there were no immediate consequences of the Benson study. The Office of Strategic Offensive and Defensive Systems (OP-97) and the Naval Communications and Intelligence commands were established. Several assistant chiefs were made Assistant Deputy Chiefs of Naval Operations in order to limit the number of people with access to the vice chief and the CNO.[52] But the major issue—the organizational doctrine for OPNAV— had been left unresolved.

In 1968 the Director of the Long Range Objectives Group (OP-93) suggested to CNO Moorer that OPNAV be "organized in groups, each of which closely conforms to the organization of an outside organization which is a major communicant of the CNO."[53] OP-93's idea was to create three DCNOs for program planning, fleet readiness, and strategic plans. The first would deal with the Secretary of the Navy; the second, with the Chief of Naval Material and with the naval component commanders at the unified commands; and the third, with the Joint Chiefs. The deputy for program planning would focus on budget categories such as ship construction and operations and maintenance. The deputy for fleet readiness would be organized by warfare area—antisubmarine, amphibious assault, aviation, at-sea replenishment, and so forth. The deputy for strategic plans would be supported by a functional director whose fields conformed to those of the JCS Joint Staff directorates. A director of the Navy staff (DNS) and a director of naval analysis would assist the Chief and Vice Chief of Naval Operations. Each deputy chief would be assisted by a director of studies who would communicate directly with a director of studies and analysis reporting to the deputy for program planning.

OP-93's proposal recognized three major clients of OPNAV—the fleet, the Secretary of the Navy, and the JCS. The proposal also recognized the three primary functions of OPNAV—planning, supporting the fleet by structuring and supplying naval forces, and supporting the Secretary of the Navy as he made policy. What was interesting about the proposal, however, was its admission that the primary duty of OPNAV was to respond, not to command. As OP-93 was preparing its proposal, Admiral Bernard A. Clarey, Vice Chief of Naval Operations, asked the Systems

1128104 U.S. Navy

President Lyndon B. Johnson and CNO Thomas H. Moorer visit the nuclear-powered attack aircraft carrier *Enterprise* (CVAN-65), November 1967.

Analysis Division to study OPNAV's organization yet again. OP-96 found the same shortcomings with OPNAV:

- OPNAV is too large. There are about 1100 officers alone.

- The rank structure is too top heavy. . . .

- There is a great deal of duplication of effort.

- The span of control of the CNO/VCNO is too great. . . .

- For many, if not most, complex issues there is no clear line of responsibility. . . .

- The current OPNAV organization is not structured by either mission or weapons platform but rather by a mixture. . . .

- The fact that Washington duty is a virtual prerequisite for selection to flag rank causes many billets to be designated as captain billets which could be filled by more junior officers.[54]

Under a mandate to recommend only those changes which would cause "minimum disruption of OPNAV," the OP-96 study group ran into a problem.[55] What if its study suggested major changes? Members of the study group thought the problem was solved when they found "Admiral

Benson's notes of his briefing for SECNAV."[56] They were excited about the organizational alternatives studied by the Benson Task Force but they soon discovered that the alternatives were never presented in the final report. The OP-96 group concluded that the Benson study omitted the alternatives because any real change in OPNAV "would require time and legislation" and would therefore "be vulnerable to attack."[57] Nevertheless, the OP-96 officers recommended that the Chief of Naval Material be made a deputy chief for resources and that, consequently, the DCNO positions for Logistics (OP-04) and Development (OP-07) be eliminated.

What OP-96 proposed was a gradual change in OPNAV, with a director of the Navy staff under the Vice Chief of Naval Operations. Assistant directors would be appointed for manpower, JCS matters, communications and intelligence, general purpose forces, sealift, oceanography, and strategic offensive and defensive forces. An office of an assistant director for program appraisal would generate long-range objectives and systems analyses of ongoing programs. In making this proposal, the Systems Analysis Division was heavily influenced by the OP-93 (Long Range Objectives Group) study and by a staff reorganization of the Royal Navy, which had just become effective. What is so interesting about the OP-96 effort is that it reveals an incredible absence of institutional memory. The Benson Task Force put together a detailed, thoughtful study. By the time Admiral Moorer was considering reorganization, the ideas generated by the Benson study had lost their influence, despite the fact that Benson had explained them to a number of senior flag officers.

The McNamara years (1961–1968) were a whirlwind time for OPNAV. As one commentator said, "From 1961 to 1964 McNamara proved himself an unrivaled master at establishing firm civilian control over the massive Pentagon program."[58] To attain that level of control he expanded the size and authority of the Office of the Secretary of Defense. Between 1962 and 1969, for example, the OSD staff increased by almost fifty percent, as did the staff of the office of the Joint Chiefs of Staff. Organizations under the control of the Defense secretary or the JCS, such as the Defense Intelligence Agency, the Defense Supply Agency, the Defense Communications Agency, and the Defense Contract Audit Agency, also increased in size. During that same period, in contrast, the size of the Office of the Secretary of the Navy decreased by over a third, OPNAV stayed the same, and the headquarters of the Marine Corps grew by over twenty-five percent.[59] McNamara also used his authority to establish his office as the center of defense policy making and overall military command. He yielded to no one except the President.

As Secretary of Defense, McNamara imposed programming practices on the services through the use of the Planning, Programming, and Budgeting System. He understood the difference between data collection as a means of tracking expenditures and data collection as a means of discovering what an organization is doing and of controlling that organization. Later secretaries altered McNamara's system, but they did not abandon programming as the major tool of implementing force planning decisions. Budgets, for example, are still expressed in terms of Total Obligational Authority, and in the PPBS process the emphasis on the multiyear defense plan continues. Programming dramatically changed OPNAV's relationships with the rest of the Navy. OPNAV ceased to be the staff of the Navy's senior commander, becoming instead the staff of a deputy chief executive whose major responsibility was support of the operating forces.

Under McNamara everything changed—planning, the programming process, the relative authority of the Chief of Naval Operations, and the means by which major systems were procured. In 1964, for example, Assistant Secretary of the Air Force Robert Charles introduced the concept of Total Package Procurement. McNamara adopted it and forced it on the other services. Total Package Procurement meant that "contractors competing for a weapon-system award were required to submit binding price bids for the entire program—*production as well as development*—before the award was made."[60] It looked like a great innovation. But the concept encouraged the services to enter into wholesale production deals that left no escape if there were problems with the firm that won the contract.

Before the Second World War, for example, the Navy usually built the lead ship of a class in a government yard. The cost and schedule for this first ship was then used to gauge the performance of private shipyards. In the 1950s, when government shipyards focused on modernization of the fleet and new construction was left to private firms, the Navy often parceled out ships of the same class among different yards to encourage competition. Under Total Package Procurement, private firms were induced to bid on major systems by the promise that the low bidder would get the whole package, from initial design to final construction. The idea was a disaster for the Navy because it shifted responsibility for design work from the systems commands to private firms, leaving the Navy dependent on a few major construction yards. As Norman Friedman noted in his detailed study of destroyer designs, total procurement of the DD-963 type meant that "a company with no previous preliminary design experience had to create a new destroyer design from scratch."[61]

* * *

Melvin R. Laird, Secretary of Defense, 1969–1973.

By the end of the McNamara regime, OPNAV looked like a patchwork organization, the morale of senior officers was extremely low, and the future of the office was in doubt. The policies of President Richard Nixon's Defense secretary, Melvin Laird, however, both improved the management system left behind by McNamara and assuaged the battered morale of senior military leaders. Laird employed what former Assistant Secretary of Defense Lawrence Korb has termed "participatory management." According to Korb, "Laird looked primarily to the military services and the Chiefs for the design of the force structure. The civilian systems analysts were limited to evaluating and reviewing the military's proposals."[62] The new secretary did "not attempt to exercise control of details in the defense budget. Once he established an annual budget, and 'set fences' around specific program categories within the budget, Laird allowed the services wide latitude in structuring the categories."[63]

Laird used other tactics to avoid antagonizing the services. He began the process of leavening cost effectiveness analyses with political, fiscal and manpower factors. It was the difference between telling (as McNamara had done) and explaining; it was part of Laird's strategy of governing the services by listening to them and representing them in Congress. Laird allowed "the military to appeal his decisions whenever and wherever they wished," and he even permitted them to procure or develop systems with doubtful value in cost-effective terms—the B-1 bomber, for example.[64] Finally, Laird gave the services fiscal guidance at the beginning of the PPBS cycle instead of at the end. Under this system, the services bore "the burden of making the tough choices about which areas to cut during the 37.2 per cent reduction in the real level of defense spending which occurred in the 1969-75 period."[65]

Laird revealed his skill as an organizational politician when he simultaneously reduced military expenditures and tightened OSD's control over service acquisition. By creating the Defense Systems Acquisition Review Council (DSARC), he gained control over major systems development. As Laird's deputy, former industrialist David Packard, told the service secretaries, "The primary responsibility for the acquisition and management of our major systems must rest with the individual Services." Yet he also explained that, as Deputy Secretary of Defense, he was "most anxious of insuring, before we approve transitioning through the critical milestones of the acquisition of a major system, that all facets of the acquisition process are properly considered."[66] DSARC complemented the Five Year Defense Program that was part of the Planning, Programming, and Budgeting System by giving a council of assistant Defense secretaries the chance to review major programs before so many resources were committed that any decision to cut off those resources would have become organizationally impossible. Creating the council was a way of getting OSD in on the "ground floor" of development programs and then subjecting them to continual OSD assessment.

Laird had to be a skilled Pentagon politician. The Nixon administration had pledged to reduce defense spending, end the draft, and leave the war in Vietnam to the Vietnamese. The services wanted to keep the draft, win the war, and rebuild inventories depleted by combat and age. That Laird accomplished the administration's goals without seriously antagonizing the service secretaries and chiefs is a testimony to his abilities. One of those abilities was an appreciation of the symbolic side to leadership. McNamara had outworked, outargued, and outmaneuvered the service chiefs. Laird's style was very different. Vice Admiral William P. Mack, Deputy Assistant Secretary of Defense for Manpower and Reserve Affairs, under Laird, commented:

> [I]t was thought by navy officials, officers, that you really weren't working right unless you worked at least ten hours a day, seven days a week. . . . And when you wrote a paper or a speech it had to be nitpicked to death . . . that's the way paper work and administration were done, particularly in the Navy Department. I'd been through this for years, and I didn't think it was the way it should be, so to me it was quite a clean breeze to come to the Defense Department and find . . . that it was staffed at the very highest level by businessmen who didn't believe this, who thought that if you couldn't do your work in eight hours a day on five days, perhaps occasionally six, you weren't doing it right. In other words, you weren't delegating responsibility properly.[67]

The key term is "delegating." It did not matter so much that Laird delegated the duty of finding ways to cut spending instead of increasing it. What really counted was that Laird and his associates in OSD recognized an area of service responsibility and respected it, making sure that the services knew why OSD was doing so.

As far as OPNAV was concerned, things were getting worse—organizationally. At least that was what a "Special Review" by the Naval Audit Service concluded at the beginning of 1969. Audit Service investigators reported that they had

> been unable to identify, at any level below the immediate office of the Chief of Naval Operations, a unit, group, or board, where a truly objective decision is made for the best interest of the Navy, particularly with regard to allocations of available funds to the various programs. . . . The final recommendations to CNO for program priority rests [*sic*] with the Chief of Naval Operations Advisory Board (CAB).[68]

But the deputy chiefs and the assistant chiefs who sat on the board settled their major differences through back-stage bargaining *before* the meetings. Hence the board did not base its decisions after "an objective determination of priority need."[69] To do well in the bargaining sessions, "each DCNO/ACNO considers it his responsibility to be knowledgeable with respect to substantially all Navy actions."[70] Unfortunately, the need for intelligence on what other offices were planning and programming led to a wasteful duplication of staffs.

This requirement for intelligence on competing offices within the organization drove the deputy chiefs to demand reports from the fleet and from the Chief of Naval Material, burying OPNAV offices in paper. The Audit Service estimated that OPNAV received more than four times as much paper as was necessary.[71] But the paper was the essential fuel for the necessary studies. Because decisions about programs were reached through an essentially political process, the parties to the process (essentially a zero-sum game, especially under the cost-cutting imposed by OSD) needed not only information but also what is referred to in political lobbying literature as "partisan analysis"—studies showing the virtue of one position, or alternative, over another. Given the way OPNAV worked, studies were imperative. They were also wasteful:

> (1) Personnel are selected for Special Studies on the basis of rank and not on the basis of expertise in their individual specialty. (2) The basis of the need for Studies and the Study Objectives are vague. (3) Studies in progress are not adequately monitored. (4) There is little post evaluation of Study results and no evidence of concern for cost effectiveness.[72]

The auditors added another complaint: "A major portion of the total

OPNAV effort is devoted to processing JCS papers."[73] In fiscal year 1968 alone, OP-06 (Plans and Policy) processed almost 18,000 JCS papers, many of which required an immediate reply. The presence of a larger Joint Staff, allowed by the 1958 DOD Reorganization Act, seemed to confirm former CNO Burke's fears that the Joint Chiefs would become a drain on both the CNO and OPNAV.

The Audit Service observed that "detail to OPNAV appears to have an adverse effect on morale and encourages separation from the Service."[74] High ranking officers became involved in "clerical type detail and other routine functions not related to Navy policy, or not requiring any military expertise."[75] To compound matters, just as officers had mastered their office duties, they were rotated out of their positions. And those new officers entering OPNAV often lacked sufficient training in administrative and fiscal matters.[76]

Navy auditors sharply criticized OPNAV for its lack of a "centralized management of Logistics within the Navy," noting that they "have been unable to arrive at a clear definition of what the logistics role of OP-04 is intended to be."[77] OP-04 was supporting the other deputy chiefs instead of formulating policy. Moreover, the Naval Material Command had "never developed any management capability related to Air programs," and the systems commands were "operating substantially according to the former Bureau organizational lines and this promotes bypassing in the reporting chain."[78] Finally, the Audit Service noted that the "relationship and relative responsibilities of the program sponsor and the appropriation sponsor" were "not entirely clear."[79] That is, the command links between OPNAV and the systems commands were not clear.

The 1969 audit exposed all the cracks in OPNAV's structure, and showed that the Chief of Naval Operations was losing charge of his own staff. Authority in OPNAV was fragmented, and lines of authority crisscrossed and overlapped. The Naval Material Command was not really managing the systems commands, in part because it was not fully integrated into OPNAV. As the naval auditors argued, "the organization and the functions of OPNAV should be restricted to policy, coordination, and direction" and the "subordinate commands should be used for operational detail."[80]

The reactions of the deputy chiefs and the assistant chiefs to the audit report were "in the majority of instances . . . unfavorable."[81] The DCNO for Development, for example, argued that the competition among deputy chiefs for funds was "not harmful," while the DCNO for Logistics maintained that duty in the Pentagon was essential for a successful career. The DCNO for Air disagreed with the auditors' claim that OPNAV service was frustrating, and he also asserted that time spent on

JCS papers kept the Chief of Naval Operations involved in JCS decisions. The prospect of consolidating the Naval Material Command and OP-04 was "appalling" to the DCNO for Logistics.[82] As the Assistant VCNO, Director of Naval Administration, had observed in a memo to his boss, the opposition to the suggestions and analysis of the Audit Service would keep the Vice Chief of Naval Operations from making any changes.[83] Put another way, no reorganization could be successful without the approval of officers who were the nominal subordinates to the Chief of Naval Operations. OPNAV was, indeed, a loose confederation of offices, which competed among themselves for the CNO's support.

6

Zumwalt: Reviving the Service

Admiral Elmo Zumwalt was appointed CNO in the summer of 1970. As far as the Navy was concerned, Zumwalt's appointment was one of the most important acts by Secretary Laird during the first Nixon administration. He was young, ambitious, enthusiastic, intelligent, and aggressive. Zumwalt, however, was not CNO Moorer's choice as his successor, because the youthful surface officer had already earned a reputation for being unorthodox. As expected (and in some quarters feared), Zumwalt took office "committed to changing Navy policy in a variety of areas" and convinced that the Navy "was confused about its justification for existence."[1] His policy initiatives in matters of discipline, naval dress, race relations, naval strategy, and cost overruns in warship construction are described elsewhere, most notably in the admiral's memoirs.

Even before Zumwalt's tenure began, naval leaders had been concerned about calls for both Defense and Navy reorganization. In 1969, for example, the Nixon administration had commissioned a "Blue Ribbon Defense Panel" to study the organization and administration of the Defense Department. CNO Moorer had carefully tracked the panel's discussions through OP-06 (Plans and Policy). The panel had made several recommendations to the President. One suggested reducing the staffs in the service headquarters, the office of the service secretaries, the Joint Staff, the Office of the Secretary of Defense, and the unified commands because the existing situation encouraged "excessive paper work and coordination, delay, duplication and unnecessary expense." A second advised that "management throughout the supply, maintenance and transportation systems of the Department [of Defense]" be better integrated. A third proposed reorganizing the unified command staffs so that they were really under the control of the CINCs. A fourth called for removing the Navy's systems commands from OPNAV and giving them to a line command (or commands).[2] Indeed, like the Symington Committee of 1960, the Blue Ribbon Defense Panel suggested a wholesale reorganization of the Defense Department. Although the panel stopped short of recommending service unification, it nevertheless offered a list of proposals that was just too comprehensive for the Secretary of Defense to accept as a package.

But that did not mean the services would escape the danger of serious organizational reform dictated from above. In October 1970, the Committee on Government Operations of the House of Representatives argued in its report that the U.S. military experience in Vietnam showed that the logistics organizations of the services needed reform. Secretary of Defense Laird noted, in a letter to the committee's chairman, that the Blue Ribbon Defense Panel had reached a similar conclusion, and that the Department of Defense had already acted to improve military logistics.[3] Zumwalt, aware of the pressure to reorganize the Defense Department, including the services, established his own "Organizational Review Panel" in OPNAV soon after becoming CNO.[4]

In August 1970, while waiting for his panel's report, Zumwalt established the Navy Decision Center, a board room where he and his vice chief and their staffs could meet regularly in closed sessions to discuss internal organizational problems. Zumwalt had already created the CNO Executive Panel (CEP), a special panel of experts from outside the Navy to supplement organizations such as the CNO Advisory Board. To support the CEP, Zumwalt set up a special staff office, OP-00K. The Ad Hoc Priorities Analysis Group, formed in September, assisted OP-00K in developing "a clear statement of a Navy concept suitable for use in the next four years for reshaping the Navy, using it so that civilian members of the Office of the Secretary of Defense, White House, and Congress would more clearly understand the Navy's mission, purpose and vital importance to U.S. national objectives."[5]

Part of the problem in clarifying the Navy's role in furthering national objectives came as a result of the Navy's preoccupation with the budgetary process. This was evident in an OP-03G (Fleet Operations) memo to OP-090 (Program Planning), which noted: "Practically the entire OPNAV organization is tuned, like a tuning fork, to the vibrations of the budgetary process. . . . [T]here is a vast preoccupation with budgetary matters at the expense of considering planning, or readiness or requirements, or operational characteristics or any of the other elements contributing to the ability of the Fleets to fight."[6] The CNO shared this view of OPNAV, and OP-00K's assignment revealed the essence of Zumwalt's organizational strategy: creating a sense of mission within the Navy by giving it new ideas and controlling OPNAV by manipulating concepts and images. OP-00K gradually became the CNO's immediate staff, a "kitchen cabinet" within OPNAV.

As a former aide to the admiral commented later, Zumwalt "had an essential distrust of a bureaucracy."[7] This trait is precisely what could be expected of a talented, successful Navy "operator." As Zumwalt apparently suspected, however, his operator's credentials were not strong enough to secure his position as the Navy's chief officer. Zumwalt had never commanded one of the numbered fleets, and unlike predecessors such as Burke, his operational command experience did not compensate for his relative youth.

1144743 U.S. Navy

Admiral Elmo R. Zumwalt, Jr., Chief of Naval Operations (1970-1974), speaks to the press during his first official visit to the Atlantic Fleet in Norfolk, Virginia.

A point often forgotten is that Burke and Zumwalt, both relatively junior when appointed CNO, could not use the same techniques to first establish their legitimacy and then use that legitimacy to reform the Navy. Burke was able to make substantial changes. During his first four years in office, the Navy switched from analog to digital control technology, developed a submerged intermediate-range ballistic missile system, and fielded major missile air defense systems. But Burke had moved cautiously and was careful to win allies in the service before making controversial decisions. Because of his work in OP-23 (Organizational Research and Policy) in the forties, Burke was identified as an independent Navy man, and drew on that image to win support from his fellow officers.

Zumwalt had no such image. Many of his peers regarded him as a decidedly "political" appointee, and their unease at his appointment denied him command authority. Moreover, Zumwalt's belief that multiple crises were seriously threatening the Navy prompted him to move quickly to effect change. As a result, he sent a cluster of "Z-grams," messages directly from the CNO to the fleet, stating changes in policies that the CNO had real control over (e.g., dress codes and race relations). Moorer, Zumwalt's predecessor, had begun reform in these fields, but he had worked gradually and quietly through the chain of command. Zumwalt bypassed the chain of command and spoke directly to the fleet, calling his action the "least-worst" choice.[8] Zumwalt's methods, however, may be interpreted as a means of making the fleet dependent on the CNO and thereby establishing the CNO's authority both within the fleet and within OPNAV.

In November 1970 members of the OPNAV Organizational Review Panel briefed Zumwalt on the results of their study. Most suggestions resembled the proposals developed by earlier studies, particularly the Benson report of 1966. The panel proposed that OPNAV eliminate the DCNO positions of Logistics and Development and absorb the Naval Material Command to perform those duties. A second suggestion, which Zumwalt approved, elevated the authority and rank of the Director of Navy Program Planning to a principal assistant to the CNO. A third idea focused all nuclear warfare planning with the DCNO for Plans and Policy.[9] If implemented, these proposals could not increase the size of OPNAV's staff, because the Secretary of Defense had ordered the service secretaries to reduce headquarters (including OPNAV) civilian and military personnel by fifteen percent in September.[10] However, it was also clear that the Secretary of Defense would not contravene Zumwalt's efforts to reorganize OPNAV.

The battle over centralization of functions in the Defense Department continued, however. In January 1971 Deputy Secretary of Defense David Packard announced that he and Secretary Laird, contrary to the recommendation of the Blue Ribbon Defense Panel, did not "intend to establish a single Defense-wide Logistics Command at this time." However, they promulgated a "set of logistics systems policy objectives" that eventually formed the basis of a DOD Logistics Systems Plan.[11] In response to "an OSD drafted Blueprint for logistics change and to the numerous memoranda coming from OSD," Vice Admiral George E. Moore, the Vice Chief of Naval Material, had recommended the formation of a logistics policy committee.[12] Composed of logistics specialists from the services, this committee developed its own cross-service logistics plan. Upon its completion, the plan was viewed by Vice Admiral Moore and others as an effective means of blocking any OSD changes that the services regarded as threatening.[13] But Deputy Secretary Packard withheld from the Logistics Systems Policy Committee the authority to set the terms of the plan. As an OP-06 (Plans and Policy) study noted, "a common Service view that the [Committee] would provide Service control of the logistics systems changes has not emerged."[14]

OP-06 viewed Secretary Laird's concept of "participatory management" as "participation when you do what they [DOD] want." Whether this was a fair assessment or not, the point is that Zumwalt attempted internal reforms while, from the Navy's standpoint, OSD was encroaching on service prerogatives and undermining service autonomy. Like his predecessors, Zumwalt faced pressure from above and below. The pressure from below was not only a resistance to Zumwalt's policies in areas like race relations and military demeanor, but also opposition from high ranking officers like Vice Admiral Rickover. Rickover ran a significant portion of the Navy directly, or indirectly, and he was virtually immune to CNO control. Zumwalt had tried to "bargain with Rickover . . . , but Rickover — probably seeing that the deal was not a prerequisite to achieving his goals — refused."[15] In a sense, Rickover was acting logically because OPNAV lacked the discipline necessary to achieve his goals. Rickover felt that both his success and that of the Navy's nuclear power program depended on his demonstrated political skills. Zumwalt did not see himself as a threat to Rickover, but Rickover regarded him (and openly accused him of being) a political admiral. Zumwalt believed he had no choice but to act as he did, however. The CNO had to be political to be effective; the nature, or character, of the Navy's organization required it.

1144737 U.S. Navy

Admiral Zumwalt meets crewmen on board amphibious assault ship *Guadalcanal* (LPH-7) at Norfolk, Virginia, July 1970.

To gain some control over OPNAV, Zumwalt moved on three fronts simultaneously. First, he tried to invigorate strategic and tactical thinking by placing more emphasis on electronic warfare, antiship missiles, and on professional development such as the programs of study at the Naval War College. He wanted to win the support of officers with innovative ideas. Second, he tried to get control of the shipbuilding budget with the high/low concept. He argued that the Navy needed to replace numerous but now worn- out ships built during the Second World War with ships that, though modern, were really not suited for the high-intensity engagements that carrier battle groups were designed for. The FFG-7-class ship, designed mainly for antisubmarine warfare in the convoy routes of the North Atlantic, was a product at the lower end of Zumwalt's high/low operations intensity spectrum. Another product, the sea control ship, or small carrier, was never built, largely because its construction was not cost-effective when compared with the existing and planned large carriers.[16] But the high/low approach was imaginative and, if only imperfectly, it addressed the Navy's need for ships in a time of fiscal austerity. Third, Zumwalt reorganized OPNAV.

As a CNO attempting reform, Zumwalt could not ignore the trend toward earlier career specialization that began during the Second World War. The Navy had changed drastically since the days before 1941. Then the concept of a general line officer, broadly trained and by mid-career capable of taking on a variety of assignments, made sense. The growth of technology made the notion of the "general line" obsolescent, however, and the Navy gradually developed very different communities of line officers. In the 1930s, for example, Annapolis graduates could not begin aviation training right after graduation. Regardless of their qualifications for flight training, they served for two years in the fleet. Then once they earned their wings, naval aviators were required to fly several types of aircraft under different conditions before specializing in one area. A carrier pilot had to spend a year or two flying floatplanes from battleships, or long-range seaplanes from tenders, before joining a carrier squadron. This policy gave younger officers a broad base of experience so that, when they reached higher command, they would understand the diversity of the Navy's forces.

Necessarily abandoned during the war, that policy was not revived after the war largely because younger officers took longer to master the newer, more complex specialties. By the mid-1950s the Navy found that allowing officers to specialize early in their careers was the most cost-effective approach to training. Aviation grew more specialized because of the unique training needed just to enable young fliers to maneuver sophisticated jet aircraft on and off carrier decks safely. Nuclear propulsion turned the submarine warfare community into a highly specialized, rather isolated branch of the service. Zumwalt could not arrest these trends, but he did search for something that would pull the warfare communities (submarine, surface, and air) back together.

In March 1971 the CNO finally organized the deputies along the "four forces" concept as created by the Benson Task Force. (See Figure 4.) The title of the Deputy Chief of Naval Operations for Fleet Operations and Readiness (OP-03) changed to DCNO for Surface, later Surface Warfare. The DCNO for Air inherited all the offices in the old OP-03 that programmed aviation activities. The Deputy Chief of Naval Operations for Submarines (OP-02), later Submarine Warfare, was established. Without specific permission from Congress to create OP-02, Zumwalt eliminated OP-07 (Development), redesignating it Director of Research, Development, Test and Evaluation, so that the number of deputy chiefs remained constant.[17] This move represented a major change in focus because it shifted the OPNAV organization further away from functional lines and more toward warfare, or platform, communities. OP-01 (Manpower and Naval Reserve), OP-04 (Logistics), and OP-06 (Plans and Policy) were the only DCNO offices whose interests stretched across the platform communities.

In effect, Zumwalt placated the three major warfare communities by vesting each with permanent representation in OPNAV. Integration of these communities was achieved in the directorates headed by deputies of the Vice Chief of Naval Operations: Director of Navy Program Planning (OP-090); Director of Tactical Electromagnetic Programs (OP-093); Director of Antisubmarine Warfare Programs (OP-095); a new Director of Research, Development, Test and Evaluation (OP-098); and Director of Naval Education and Training (OP-099).

These directorates under the vice chief became the CNO's real staff. While Zumwalt reassured the deputy chiefs in January 1971 that they would retain the authority to manage programs over which they had cognizance, he also explained that the directorates were meant to "provide a systems overview . . . to ensure that . . . the Navy's resources are correctly allocated to those systems which provide the Navy with the best possible operational capability."[18] When it became clear to Zumwalt that OPNAV was too large to use effectively as a staff, he began creating his staff-within-a-staff.

As part of this process, Zumwalt disbanded OP-097, the directorate for Strategic Offensive and Defensive Systems, and shifted its functions and personnel to OP-06 in June 1971.[19] In August 1971 Zumwalt established the Fiscal Management Division (OP-92) under the Director of Navy Program Planning.[20] This was part of his plan to focus, in OP-090, enough staff support to enable him to review and evaluate all major Navy

OFFICE OF THE CHIEF OF NAVAL OPERATIONS, 1971

Figure 4

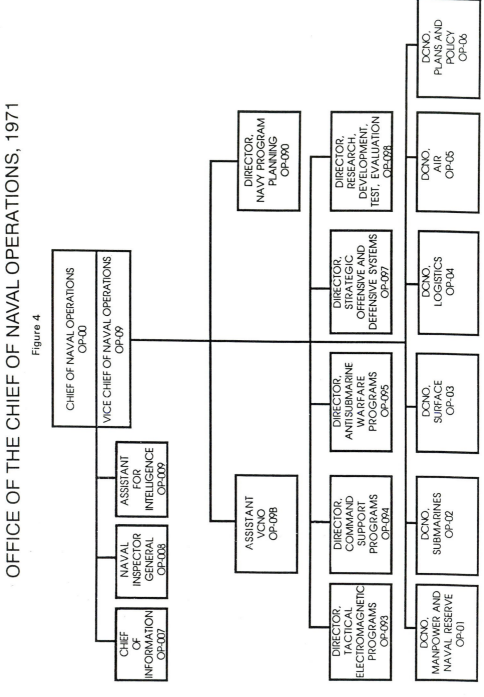

programs. Another part of his plan was to make the Systems Analysis Division (OP-96), both a source of ideas and a source of intelligence on what the deputy chiefs were planning. For example, Vice Admiral Worth H. Bagley, Director of Navy Program Planning, told the deputy chiefs and the Chief of Naval Material, "Ultimately, I expect OP-96 to provide Study Project Officers for all studies in the CNO program, insofar as this is agreeable."[21]

Zumwalt continued to strengthen the directorates under the vice chief in 1972. In March he combined OP-92 with the Office of the Deputy Chief of Naval Material for Programs and Financial Management, thereby linking the fiscal control divisions of OPNAV and the Naval Material Command.[22] That summer another board studying fleet staff organizations recommended eliminating the training commands on the East and West coasts, and merging the Antisubmarine Force, Atlantic, with the Second Fleet based in Norfolk.[23] That August the CNO shifted the Ship Acquisition and Improvement Division from OP-03 to OP-090 (Navy Program Planning).[24]

Zumwalt wanted to give the Navy influence in offices outside those normally staffed by Navy officers, and he also wanted to begin creating a leadership cadre for the future. In August, Zumwalt directed the Chief of Naval Personnel to establish a "small pool of exceptional young officers capable of filling key Washington slots (outside of Navy/JCS/ISA) that open up from time to time where no billets exist." Zumwalt wanted these six officers under the control and supervision of OP-96. He also directed Naval Personnel and OP-96 to "institute a system for tracking the subsequent assignment of these officers, to ensure strong consideration is given to future shore duty assignments in key Washington area billets."[25]

During November 1972 Zumwalt continued to vest more power with the directorates. He shifted "mission and functions pertaining to aircraft carriers in the Fleet Modernization Program" from OP-05 to the new Ship Acquisition and Improvement Division in OP-090. At the same time he eliminated the office of the Program Coordinator for Nuclear-powered Carriers in OP-05, transferring its mission to OP-090.[26] The Secretary of the Navy approved the transfer of reserve programs from OP-01 to the Director of Naval Reserve (OP-09R), who formally received sponsorship authority in April 1973.[27] The directorate for Tactical Electromagnetic Programs was abolished, and its functions were shifted to OP-095, renamed the Office of Antisubmarine Warfare and Tactical Electromagnetic Programs.[28] The CNO Executive Board recognized the shift of authority from the deputy chiefs to the directorates under the vice chief in April when it handed down a decision requiring the deputy chiefs to get permission from the CNO before making statements of force level requirements, ship and aircraft characteristics, characteristics of weapons systems whose development and procurement costs crossed certain thresholds, and modernization decisions for major weapons systems.[29]

Zumwalt had already hired a consulting firm, Organization Resources Counselors, Inc., to study OPNAV, and he had also solicited suggestions, through OP-96, from Rear Admiral Tyler F. Dedman, Assistant Vice Chief of Naval Operations and Director of Naval Administration.[30] The firm's study (later referred to as the Beaumont Study) was presented to Zumwalt in May 1973. Its conclusions read like a list of symptoms:

- The lines of accountability and responsibility within OPNAV and CNO's major related areas of responsibility are unclear. . . . At any given point in time it is almost impossible to identify one single individual who is responsible for a project, program or process.[31]

- [I]n the area of Program Coordinator/Project Manager, the massive duplication of channels of communications, lines of approval, access to financial resources, etc. make it extremely difficult to identify who is responsible, even though there are countless documents formally establishing authority.[32]

- The Navy's proclivity to create special units to get things done is detrimental to the integrity of any management system.[33]

- [A]llocation of resources across the many competing claimants is based on a highly complex system of personal priorities and negotiations.[34]

- Currently, OPNAV can be viewed as organized into a number of "little Navies." Each of these units attempts to remain an independent and autonomous whole, fighting to keep its boundaries (mission) intact, even to the point of departure from CNO's stated objectives. In the process, each unit attempts to acquire the organizational aspects, skills and capabilities of the others, thus remaining well-equipped for adversary proceedings even with OPNAV itself.[35]

- [B]ecause of the crisis nature of the management process, there is a tendency for OPNAV to reach into and run and direct many of the activities in subordinate commands.[36]

This list was a powerful indictment and repeated many of the observations found in earlier studies. A review committee, chaired by former VCNO Admiral James S. Russell (Ret.), was not quite sure what to do with the study, and recommended only evolutionary changes in OPNAV's organization.

Part of the Navy's problem—and Zumwalt's—was the growth of special projects offices. This management technique, first established in 1955 for the Fleet Ballistic Missile Program (Polaris) was so successful that later CNOs and chiefs of Naval Material created other project offices

1147451 U.S. Navy

The Joint Chiefs of Staff meet at the Pentagon in January 1971. *Left to right*: Admiral Zumwalt, Chief of Naval Operations; General William C. Westmoreland, Army Chief of Staff; Admiral Moorer, Chairman of the JCS; General John D. Ryan, Air Force Chief of Staff; and General Leonard F. Chapman, Jr., Commandant of the Marine Corps.

to push through development and acquisition projects in emergency cases. By 1965 the Secretary of Defense had ordered the services to use these management organizations for *all* major acquisition projects. This directive struck at the CNO's authority to control the bureaus and systems commands. By the time Zumwalt became CNO, a special projects office manager was concerned with meeting DOD deadlines set by the Defense Systems Acquisition Review Council—not with whether his program was tied to the initiatives of the current CNO.

Moreover, because many projects continued through the terms of several CNOs, project managers with many years of experience could deal directly and expertly with both OSD and Congress. The scope of the management problem is apparent from the numbers. Between 1955 and 1973, the chiefs of Naval Material designated twenty-two special projects. By 1976, the average life span of these projects was almost six years, or two years longer than the expected term of the Chief of Naval Operations. Thirty-one special projects in the Naval Ship Systems Command and 36 in the Naval Air Systems Command had been established, and 18 projects in each command still existed in 1973.[37]

Not all projects had the kind of visibility and status given to the Polaris project, the first special projects office. Nor did they operate under the same conditions. The special projects office for Polaris reported to a special oversight and review committee headed by the CNO (then Arleigh Burke) and the Secretary of the Navy. Most of the project offices in 1973 reported only to their sponsors in OPNAV and up the chain of command in the systems commands. Coordination across projects and programs was the responsibility of the Naval Material Command and OPNAV. However, as the Organization Resources Counselors' study showed, the Naval Material Command lacked authority and OPNAV was so splintered that project managers were on their own. To protect their resources, they cultivated support in OPNAV and in Congress, constructing alliances directly with OPNAV and congressional staffs. This situation led Secretary of Defense James D. Schlesinger to note that "if service resistance is really entrenched, it cannot be overcome."[38] Schlesinger's problem was that he dealt with program managers only through the reviews of the Defense Systems Acquisition Review Council. Those reviews focused on the ability of program managers to meet schedule and performance milestones. Money for these special programs came from the services, which were supposed to review the programs to verify that they did in fact contribute to service goals. Unfortunately, neither the Secretary of the Navy nor the CNO controlled the Planning, Programming, and Budgeting System within the Navy. Because programming was dominated by the warfare area DCNOs, there was no way for OSD to hold senior service officials responsible for integrating ongoing programs with DOD goals.

* * *

By the end of 1973 Zumwalt had just about lost the influence necessary to implement further internal reform. That December he faced yet another demand by the Office of the Secretary of Defense to pare the service headquarters staff. In a memo to Secretary of the Navy John W. Warner, Zumwalt suggested that the Navy respond by abolishing the Naval Material Command thereby avoiding a restructuring of OPNAV. Admiral Isaac C. Kidd, Jr., Chief of Naval Material, concurred.[39] But Secretary of Defense Schlesinger did not appreciate the effort, and in April 1974 ordered personnel cuts in OPNAV and in the Marine Corps headquarters. He also ordered Secretary Warner to combine the Naval Ordnance Systems Command with the Naval Ship Systems Command to form the Naval Sea Systems Command. In June, when Zumwalt had lost favor with the White House, the directorate for Ship Acquisition and Improvement (OP-097) was abolished, and its divisions were returned to OPs 02, 03, 04 and 05.[40]

As a CNO, Admiral Elmo Zumwalt was either admired or hated by senior Navy officers. His actions provoked strong, emotional responses within the Navy and within Congress. He approached OPNAV with a combination of compromise and aggressiveness. He gave the warfare communities their separate organizations within OPNAV, but he also increased significantly the power of the directorates that reported to the

Vice Chief of Naval Operations. At the end of Zumwalt's term, OP–090 had divisions capable of systematic program analysis, using a Navy-wide automated data processing and reporting system. By the summer of 1974, Zumwalt's staff-within-a-staff had taken permanent shape. The directorates—OPs 090, 094, 095 and 098—were Zumwalt's organizational legacy to his successors. All were staffed by competent senior officers who saw service in the directorates as a means of promotion.

To other Navy officers, Zumwalt had weakened the twin pillars of naval command authority—the chain of command and the emphasis on operations. At the time of his appointment, the admiral was quite concerned about retaining quality officers and enlisted personnel in the service and he moved aggressively to give talented younger officers responsibility and promotions. In the process, he undermined the tradition of seniority, thereby robbing himself (and his office) of some of the support he might otherwise have had from the officer corps.

Zumwalt also tried to stimulate thinking about naval operations, tactics, and strategy, and his efforts coined a vocabulary of new strategic terms, such as sea control, power projection, and peacetime presence. He created a Navy Net Assessment office in OP–96 to compare the U.S. and Soviet navies across the board, and circulated the reports of this office throughout OPNAV.[41] The short-range benefit of such innovations for Zumwalt was limited, but the long-term benefit for the Navy was substantial.[42]

When he took office, Zumwalt faced significant obstacles in his efforts to reform OPNAV and the Navy. Service morale and retention rates were extremely low. The Navy needed new modern ships, but the Secretary of Defense was under orders to reduce defense expenditures. Racial injustice and conflicts in the fleet led Zumwalt to address immediately the grievances of black sailors, but many senior officers believed he moved too quickly to force solutions on the service. Zumwalt had neither the command experience nor the network of allies in the Navy that might have helped his campaign for reform. In short, he lacked the resources necessary to sustain the kinds of changes that he proposed. Moreover, his policy initiatives often denied him the sympathy that he needed for successful reorganization. Lack of funds compounded the difficulties of reorganization because the CNO had few means to compensate those who were forced to relinquish authority.

Finally, Zumwalt ran up against the sheer size of OPNAV. In 1939, before the Navy really mobilized for the Second World War, about 125 officers worked in OPNAV. By 1970 their number had swelled to at least one thousand. A Chief of Naval Operations might run an organization of this size *if* he had the time and *if* he could rely on the special ethical and social relationship characteristic of operational command. But Zumwalt had neither. As a result, he could do no more than establish his staff-within-a-staff—the Navy directorates. Put another way, he developed bureaucratic means to deal with what was in fact a large bureaucracy.

7

Zumwalt to Lehman

Z umwalt had turned OPNAV upside down. His support of the sea control ship challenged the status of the large aircraft carrier as the center of Navy conventional forces. He had attacked the idea that all Navy surface escorts had to be first-line. He not only gave the platform communities representation in OPNAV and on the CNO Executive Panel, but also strengthened the programmers and analysts who worked directly for the Vice Chief of Naval Operations. Zumwalt also had initiated the net assessment process in OP-96 (Systems Analysis), deliberately linking intelligence specialists, analysts, and programmers at the headquarters level. The next CNO, Admiral James L. Holloway III, had to decide whether to continue and extend the changes Zumwalt began, or let organizational matters settle. He chose to do the latter.[1]

His decision was understandable. Under Zumwalt and his two successors, Holloway and Thomas B. Hayward, the Navy continued to modernize the fleet, replacing the large number of ships inherited from the massive building programs of the Second World War with fewer but more sophisticated types. As the Soviet fleet expanded and also grew more sophisticated, the pressure to stay ahead *technologically* of the opposition increased. Moreover, the war in Southeast Asia had demonstrated convincingly the importance of electronic warfare, as well as the problems associated with "staying ahead" in the twilight electronics battlefield. By Zumwalt's term, the need to modernize the Navy, coupled with the very high cost of modern weapons and sensors, forced the CNO and the Secretary of the Navy to ask the Secretary of Defense and Congress for additional funding for new ships and aircraft. Congress appeared more hostile to such requests and more aggressive toward the Defense Department and the services, but allocated a greater share of new appropriations to the Navy than to the Air Force and Army.[2]

By the mid-1970s, however, after Admiral Holloway was appointed CNO, annual inflation in the shipbuilding industry was between 15 and 20 percent, or almost four times the amount that Navy programmers estimated when they requested funds for new construction in 1972.[3] OSD was not convinced that the Navy needed additional construction appropriations and criticized the quality of Navy ship and weapons designs. Vice Admiral Eli T. Reich, then working for the Deputy Secretary of Defense, observed in February 1975, "the Navy has done an inadequate job of specifying overall ship system integration design—

Admiral James L. Holloway III, Chief of Naval Operations, 1974–1978.
1168118 U.S. Navy

systems engineering and total ship design integration have been seriously lacking in post-World War II surface ship acquisitions."[4] But with growing evidence that the Soviet fleet was planning and training to use tactical nuclear weapons in any major engagement with the U.S. Navy, the CNOs after Zumwalt were faced with the problem of how to compete with both the quantitative and qualitative arms challenges presented by Soviet naval forces.[5] For example, OPNAV's Director of Organizational Appraisal (OP–09E2), Rear Admiral Gerald E. Synhorst, told CNO Holloway that "faced with real needs to support forces which have been employed in real wars or crises (and which can be expected to be called again), the OPNAV staff and the CINCs whittle away at support for TacNucs (make-believe weapons which they don't really expect to be able to use), in favor of non-nuclear problems which are considered real, and solvable, problems."[6] In this high-pressure environment, OPNAV needed all of its resources to fend off or satisfy critics in OSD and Congress. Fleet modernization through new construction was the first priority over reorganization.

Achieving modernization was not easy. By the early 1970s the Navy was developing a layered defense of its carrier battle groups against attacks by missiles launched by Soviet bombers. The outer layer of this air defense shield was composed of F-14 fighters, each capable of engaging simultaneously up to six enemy targets with advanced Phoenix missiles. Sophisticated carrier-based electronics surveillance aircraft orbiting above the battle group controlled the movements of the fighters. The Aegis missile-firing surface ship formed the next layer of defense. With electronically steered, phased-array radar beams, the ship could monitor the middle range around the battle groups and could strike at any enemy missiles that penetrated the outer screen of fighters. The final layer of defense consisted of the less expensive short-range missiles, guns, and electronic deception equipment carried by all the ships in a battle group.

This multitiered system, now in use, was not complete in the mid-1970s; the Aegis ship was missing. Admiral Holloway wanted a nuclear-powered cruiser to accompany the new *Nimitz*-class, nuclear-powered aircraft carriers then entering the fleet. The Office of the Secretary of Defense objected to these ships on the grounds of cost. Largely at the insistence of Vice Admiral Rickover, Congress had already passed a law saying that all future "major combatant vessels" had to be nuclear-powered. Aegis became deadlocked in the dispute between OSD and Congress, and in January 1975 the Secretary of Defense decided against requesting funds for Aegis ship construction or conversion. As Rear Admiral Wayne E. Meyer, project manager for Aegis, told his superior, the Chief of the Naval Sea Systems Command, "We are simply unable to

DN-SN-84-08774 U.S. Navy

Yorktown (CG–48), equipped with the new Aegis guided missile system, steams in the Gulf of Mexico, June 1984.

accomplish sensible program planning, or useful contractual work."[7] Only when the President assured Congress that a conventionally-powered Aegis ship was needed, and the CNO, reversing his position, stated that a conventionally-powered ship would be effective, did funding for the Aegis ship survive.[8]

The struggle over Aegis illustrated not only the Navy's concern for modernization and the efforts by Congress to control major weapons systems development, but also the inevitable conflict between the CNOs and the program managers who are supposedly responsible to them. Admiral Holloway hoped to field an effective, *integrated* air defense system for the Navy's carrier battle groups. At the same time, he was as concerned as Zumwalt had been about the enormous cost of modern weapons systems. The first Aegis missile-firing cruiser cost nearly $1 billion, and the projected cost of all Aegis ships was approximately $30 billion in 1976. Rear Admiral Meyer was convinced that the ships would perform as expected in the antiair warfare role and usher in a new era of battle management, with implications in *all* warfare areas. To him, developing this advanced capability was worth the cost. But the CNO had to worry about *all* costs, for both present operations and future equipment.

In June 1979 Captain Victor Basiuk, USNR, in a paper that was part of a headquarters review analysis, termed this difference between the CNO and the project managers as a conflict between "requirements pull" and "technology push."[9] That is, the Chief of Naval Operations was concerned with meeting the needs of the fleet for cost-effective anticruise missile defense, while the project manager saw Aegis as a chance to achieve a new breakthrough in battle management. The CNO necessarily stressed deploying an affordable system. His nominally subordinate program manager, on the other hand, emphasized the system's potential. As Basiuk understood, the problem was not limited to the Aegis project. It was, instead, a general characteristic of Navy development programs, most of which had their roots not in any overall analysis of fleet or theater need, but in far more narrow concerns.

A major reason why "technology push" often overcame "requirements pull" was because the Naval Material Command had never fulfilled the intent of those who had created it as the Navy's major procurement and logistics office. In the summer of 1976, for example, the Office of Management and Budget (OMB) studied the Naval Material Command's organization. The study team discovered the following deficiencies:

- The staff of the Chief of Naval Material because its duties were not clearly defined, was involved in "matters previously carried out by the systems commands or bureaus."

• The Chief of Naval Material could not do effective planning or policy analyses.

• The lines of authority between OPNAV and NAVMAT were unclear.

• The technical capability of systems commands had eroded, and much of the technical work was performed by contractors.

• The structure of the Naval Sea Systems Command was "complex and unwieldy."

• Most project managers lacked the authority to meet the goals set for them.

• Competent line officers regarded command positions in NAVMAT and the system commands as harmful to their chance for promotion and avoided such posts.[10]

This diagnosis showed that the procurement side of the Navy lacked an effective chain of command. To succeed in such a confused command

DN-SN-85-00987 U.S. Navy

A Standard missile is fired from Aegis cruiser *Ticonderoga* (CG-47).

setting, project managers needed a secure source of support. In the case of Aegis, Rear Admiral Meyer cultivated support in Congress, in OPNAV, and in the fleet. He also asked for and got a special charter for the Aegis Shipbuilding Project, which gave him potentially sweeping powers as well as definite responsibilities. In effect, Meyer was "empire-building," but he believed that the situation left him with no alternative.

As interest revived in naval strategy, the influence of the DCNO for Plans, Policy, and Operations (OP-06) gradually increased. In early 1977, CNO Holloway transferred the responsibility for conducting and analyzing joint and naval war games from OP-090 (Program Planning) to OP-06. He also moved the billets in OP-098 (Research, Development, Test and Evaluation) that were responsible for nontechnical nuclear weapons matters to OP-06.[11] Finally, he charged OP-06 with developing a statement of the Navy's strategy—that strategy was enunciated in 1978 in Naval Warfare Publication (NWP) No. 1, "Strategic Concept of the U.S. Navy."

The statement was timely. Although initally very pro-Navy, President Jimmy Carter's appointees in the Defense Department questioned the need for a large surface Navy. In May 1977 the President announced that he would ask Congress to authorize 160 new ships for the Navy over the next five years. Within a year, however, Carter had reduced that figure by half on the advice of Secretary of Defense Harold Brown (former Secretary of the Air Force). Carter also called for "a searching organizational review" of the Defense Department, beginning another series of defense management studies. The Office of Management and Budget, which favored abolishing the positions of service secretaries and chiefs, was charged with coordinating all studies of the executive branch.[12] The Navy perceived this renewed round of defense studies as a threat to its integrity because it was pushed by OMB. To make matters worse, the Navy's strategic warfare concept was threatened by Under Secretary of Defense Robert Komer and others who advocated limiting naval operations in a major war to convoy reinforcement of NATO armies in Europe.

The Carter administration ultimately sponsored three studies of DOD organization. The first, chaired by former Secretary of the Navy Paul R. Ignatius, focused on OSD and the service headquarters.[13] The second, headed by Dr. Donald Rice, president of the Rand Corporation, considered the acquisition and programming side to DOD. The third, chaired by business executive Richard C. Steadman, looked at the national military command organization. The Rice study suggested that Secretary Brown create a special board to "direct and supervise the OSD review of the Service POMs [Program Objective Memoranda] and Budget Submissions."[14] That board, created in 1979 and named the Defense

Resources Board (DRB), would play an important role in the Navy's efforts to take advantage of the defense spending increases in the 1980s.

The Ignatius study concerned OPNAV the most because, as a consultant to the CNO observed, "over the past several years, there have been repeated cuts to the SECNAV and OPNAV staff. . . . What is badly needed is time to settle down."[15] And time was just what the Navy received. The Ignatius study recommended that the service secretaries and chiefs be retained, but did call for a smaller headquarters staff. As Ignatius began his study, OPNAV, to protect itself, followed a strategy that gave the office "the appearance of having one coordinated, integrated SECNAV/OPNAV staff. Otherwise outside agencies of higher authority such as OSD, OMB, and Congress will believe the Navy has too much redundancy in its *departmental* staff and will tend to take away some of our staff assets."[16]

Secretary of the Navy W. Graham Claytor, Jr., a member of the Defense Department committee set up to advise Ignatius, opposed any effort to move functions out of the services and into the offices of the Assistant Secretaries of Defense. Claytor took a very active approach to Navy programming and systems acquisition, and he eventually challenged Secretary Brown over the administration's policy of not funding naval expansion. An officer then in OPNAV recalled: "With the arrival of Secretary Claytor and Undersecretary Woolsey, . . . OPA [Office of Program Assessment, created in response to a Dillon Board recommendation] became very directly involved in the day-to-day program planning process. . . . The Secretariat was once again showing signs of being in charge."[17] With more influence in Claytor's hands, the Navy could indeed fend off charges that the Secretariat simply duplicated functions performed in OPNAV.

But there was more to it than that. According to a 1976 study sponsored by the Comptroller General of the United States, since the services were organized to respond to the Office of the Secretary of Defense, the problem of large service headquarters staffs was directly linked to the growing influence and demands of OSD. "As requests in the name of the Secretary of Defense are made to the military departments, each organizes and staffs itself to respond to the level of detail imposed, responding almost always by creating new offices mirroring the organizational structure of the requesting authority."[18] The Carter administration, however, did not see the connection. As Captain Donald K. Forbes, head of the National Policy and Command Organization Branch of the Strategic, Plans and Policy Division in OP–06, put it in November 1977, "I don't think we should kid ourselves by thinking we can ride through the reorganization effort and come out intact."[19] Indeed, Forbes suggested that perhaps one motivation for the President's emphasis on reorganization was to give Carter "the leverage he is seeking or, as a minimum, may divert some of DOD attention from the President's give-away policy in SALT."[20]

At the request of Ignatius, OP–06 developed papers on OPNAV and its history. One such paper argued that "no one individual knows enough about the intricacies of the work done in OPNAV to plan a proper reorganization. Thus, any attempt to reorganize will be planned by committee. All vested interests will be considered, and the new organization will look amazingly similar to the old."[21] The same paper also noted that the "CNO/VCNO tend to demand full coordination and agreement among the equal powers before making critical decisions. . . . Often, such coordination results in a watered-down position that may or may not be in the best interest of the Navy."[22] Further, "we see force and mission sponsors generating force requirements relating to their own parochial interests without regard for overall Navy need."[23] Former CNO Zumwalt had strengthened the directorates, but that move in itself had not broken the "unholy alliances" between successful programmers in OPNAV and some project managers in the systems commands who, together with industrial firms, forged their own "mini-navies."

Despite attempts by Carter to force restructuring, OPNAV's organization grew more cluttered. The directorates, such as OP–098 (Research, Development, Test and Evaluation), increased in number as officers working in areas such as training, reserve affairs, and intelligence argued that their fields cut across warfare area boundaries and so deserved representation "above" the DCNO level. As a result, OPNAV's organization chart mushroomed. (See Figure 5.)

Admiral Hayward took over as CNO in the summer of 1978, after a tour as Commander in Chief, Pacific Fleet. While in Hawaii, Hayward and his staff had developed plans, collectively called Sea Strike, for using Navy carrier battle groups against Russian bases in Siberia. That planning process had convinced Hayward of the need to revitalize the Navy—strategically and tactically. He understood what Zumwalt had grasped in 1970: the Navy needed a unifying concept around which to plan and program. Otherwise, strategic planning and long-range force planning were subordinated to the ongoing PPBS process. As historian John Hattendorf correctly observed, "Hayward sought to change . . . from a budget battle to an analysis of the strategic issues for a global maritime power."[24] By 1980 Hayward was ready to follow the implications of this strategy for the organization of OPNAV. In January he changed the name of OP–095 from Director of Antisubmarine Warfare Programs to Director of Naval Warfare. That same month he ordered the creation of the Long Range Planning Group (OP–00X), and assigned the

OFFICE OF THE CHIEF OF NAVAL OPERATIONS, 1977

Figure 5

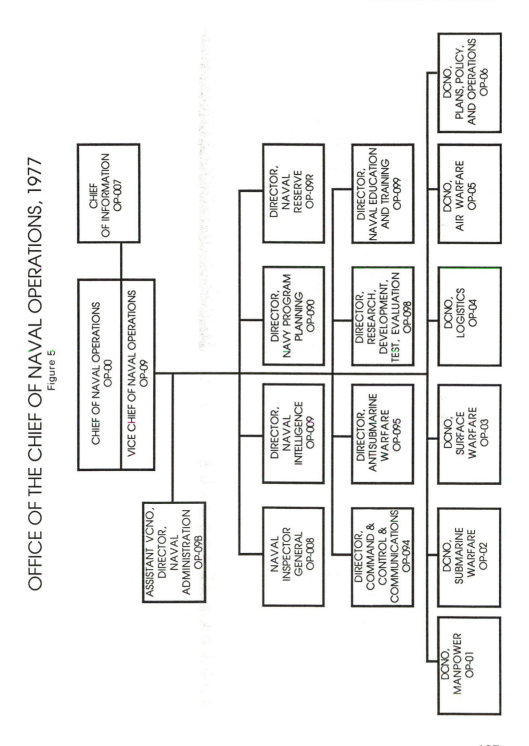

new office the task (among others) of looking for key areas of technology that might drastically affect the shape and power of the Navy in the twenty-first century. The new CNO had already created the Center for Naval Warfare Studies at the Naval War College, with one element—the Strategic Studies Group—that reported directly to him the implications of the war games conducted at the college. Hayward's goal was to create cells of bright officers who would develop what later became known as the Maritime Strategy and communicate it throughout OPNAV.[25]

A key indicator of Admiral Hayward's thinking and techniques for governing OPNAV is his elimination of the "sponsorship" in OPNAV of concepts such as sea control and power projection in the fall of 1978.[26] Hayward wanted to prevent specific platforms from appropriating certain concepts. To accomplish this, he authorized the Maritime Balance Study, which examined the way the Navy developed strategy and long-range plans.[27] The study concluded first, that the programming and budgeting "process has come to be seen as a strategy itself"; second, that research and development needed "specific mission-oriented and priority-ranked goals"; and third, that the Navy needed "a mechanism for institutionalizing its strategic planning beyond the time horizon of personnel rotation and replacement."[28] Hayward was trying to break ideas and concepts free from platforms so that he could pressure the platform communities, so strongly represented in OPNAV, to think together about missions.

Captain Basiuk's paper of June 1979 best summarized the magnitude of Hayward's task. The study described OPNAV as divided into two camps—one organized around the platform sponsors (DCNOs for submarine, surface, and air warfare); the other, around the OP-090 directorate (Program Planning).[29] Basiuk noted that "platform sponsors have been, in effect, put in charge of the development of platforms and weapon systems that go with them from . . . the development stages of R&D to their retirement from the fleet."[30] In 1979 the platform DCNOs exercised influence through their Sponsor Program Proposals (SPPs), detailed program descriptions required before programs would obtain funding.[31] Basuik recognized one positive aspect of this situation: "The Navy is a highly complex organization and platform orientation helps to reduce its fragmentation by focusing priorities and the human effort associated with them on something concrete."[32] He also saw drawbacks: "Platform orientation leads to incremental technological improvement"; worried more about their platform than what was in them, platform sponsors could "stall, and perhaps defeat," the development of new weapons that would compete with established ones; and mission sponsors, such as OP-095, had to be especially persuasive and forceful to compete with the platform sponsors for resources.[33]

CNO Thomas B. Hayward, after flying one of the Navy's new strike fighters, the F/A–18 Hornet, at the Patuxent River Naval Air Test Center, January 1980.

Although the CNO could override vetoes cast by the deputy chiefs, as Hayward did when he supported the land-attack version of the Tomahawk long-range cruise missile, such interventions were the exception given his many responsibilities. Basuik observed, "The Planning, Programming and Budgeting (PPB) process is perhaps the single most important vehicle through which the will of the CNO is projected into the shaping of priorities."[34] Unfortunately, "the budgetary process does not adequately counterbalance the power of platform sponsors," largely because OP–090 was a "microcosm of the Navy with individual loyalties finding their origins in platform constituencies."[35] The day-to-day workings of OPNAV were no secret: "Programmers from OP–090 and platform sponsors reach informal understandings behind the scenes."[36] But the informal network of alliances that crisscrossed OPNAV and spread into the Naval Material Command and the systems commands did more than steer the acquisition process. As Basuik discovered, "it is the PPB process and the studies directly or indirectly related to that process which, to a degree, marry strategic and tactical considerations with existing hardware."[37] In plain terms, OP-06 (Plans, Policy, and Operations), which considered strategic issues, was not the "focal point for the development and integration of strategic and tactical doctrines."[38]

Basiuk's paper provided insight into OPNAV because it went to the foundations of influence within that organization. Two activities mattered most in OPNAV—programming and setting the requirements for new systems—and the former was so decentralized that it was often insulated from control by the CNO. The CNO intervened in the programming process, but he lacked the time (and sometimes the knowledge) to direct it. Nor did he entirely control the requirements process because it was the systems commands that had to turn performance goals into actual hardware. PPBS placed influence in different offices as the process moved along every year. Early in the process, OSD and the Joint Chiefs worked together to draw up overall guidance for the services. Then service headquarters (OPNAV for the Navy) prepared service programs—lines of program elements with associated funding requirements. Next OSD went back and forth with the headquarters staffs until agreement was reached on how ongoing and planned programs were to be funded and implemented. That done, the service comptrollers placed budget figures alongside the program elements. The budget figures corresponded to the spending categories, such as operations and support and military construction, which Congress reviewed annually in passing on the President's budget. Once the OSD comptroller reviewed all the service budget submissions, the whole package was reviewed by the Office of Management and Budget before being sent to Congress. OMB actually compiled the President's budget and continues to do so. Only part of this long and complicated process takes place within each service where both the chief and the Secretariat staffs influence the process.

Even if he wished to, a CNO would find it almost impossible to dominate PPBS. Ship construction, for example, could stretch across the tenures of three CNOs; once begun, such programs were legitimately the province of the deputy chiefs. Consider the Aegis Shipbuilding Project. Rear Admiral Meyer, the project director, assumed responsibility for Aegis in 1970; the first Aegis ship was commissioned in 1983—after Admiral Hayward left office as CNO. Moreover, once Meyer received a special charter for the project in 1977, he was really beyond the immediate control of the CNO. The extended nature of the weapons acquisition process created a problem for CNOs who wanted to control what was produced for the Navy. If a CNO allowed performance goals for a weapon to be fixed too early, a successor would field an obsolete system. If he modified the requirement of a system to fit his vision of naval warfare, he risked wrecking the detailed, step-by-step acquisition process.

As Basiuk so ably pointed out, the Navy had painted itself into a corner. To give its headquarters staff concrete objectives, the Navy had organized one way, by platform, or warfare communities. To give the CNO some coordinating power over these communities, and to give the CNO and the Secretary of the Navy the chance to respond effectively to the Secretary of Defense, OPNAV was organized in terms of planning, programming, and budgeting. To respond to the Joint Chiefs, it set up OP-06. What the Navy lacked was the means to tie all the pieces together. Hayward thought that his strategic approach, later called the Maritime Strategy, might just do that. As a new strategy, not just a new set of tactics, the Maritime Strategy would link OP-06, the platform DCNOs (OPs 02, 03, 05), and the OP-090 programmers. It would also shift OPNAV's focus from platforms and weapons toward combined missions, in which the different elements of the Navy united to achieve larger, theater-level goals.[39] Hence, the concept of naval operations prescribed by the Maritime Strategy had definite organizational implications.

The major implication was a shift away from the programming directorate (OP-090) toward the mission-oriented office (OP-095). After Hayward changed the title of OP-095 from Director of Antisubmarine Warfare Programs to Director of Naval Warfare, he added two new divisions, one for force-level planning and a second for strike warfare. To give the restructured office some influence in programming, Hayward assigned OP-095 the task of developing the CNO Program Analysis

Memoranda, which guided the platform deputies as they drew up their annual contributions to the Navy's portion of the Five Year Defense Plan. Hayward also made OP-095 "responsible for implementing the CNO's policy for overall fleet readiness and modernization in regards to all phases of general purpose naval warfare."[40] His goal was to make the programming process swing around warfare issues that were developed by an office subordinate to the CNO and that cut across the platform deputies. It was not enough to have a systems analysis shop in OP-090 review proposals already prepared by the deputy chiefs. Hayward wanted to give the CNO the power of initiation in addition to the power of review.

8

Resurgence of the Navy Secretariat

As Hayward was reshaping the directorates, which reported to him through the Vice Chief of Naval Operations, a new presidential administration began to alter the PPBS process. The new Secretary of Defense, Caspar W. Weinberger, and his deputy, Frank C. Carlucci, informed the service secretaries that they would work "toward a system of centralized control of executive policy direction and more decentralized policy execution," where they would hold "each of the Service Secretaries responsible for the development and execution of the necessary programs and the day-to-day management of the resources under their control."[1]

The service secretaries were encouraged to express their views and participate in the decision-making process. Weinberger and Carlucci promised to improve planning throughout the PPBS cycle and to guide the services as they developed their own programs.[2] In addition, they changed the composition and responsibilities of the Defense Resources Board created by former Secretary of Defense Harold Brown to adjudicate disputes over program goals between OSD and the services. The service secretaries and chiefs were made permanent members of the board whose responsibility was extended to assist the secretary in managing "the entire revised planning, programming and budgeting process."[3]

This was a major change to the programming process. As members of the Defense Resources Board, service secretaries and chiefs were given great *potential* initiative and influence. The Secretary of Defense held them responsible for the management of their departments and encouraged them to take the initiative in making sure service programs met the guidelines outlined at the beginning of the PPBS cycle. Weinberger also changed the PPBS process itself. The Joint Chiefs of Staff continued to begin the process every fall by preparing a Joint Strategic Planning Document, a list of forces that the Joint Chiefs believed were needed to achieve the strategic goals of the United States. At the same time, however, the unified theater commanders, or CINCs, also prepared a list of programs and systems that were most important to them. At the beginning of the new year, the Office of the Secretary of Defense promulgated a draft Defense Guidance that was reviewed by the services and the Joint Chiefs. Once the reviews were complete, the Defense Resources Board met for the first time in the PPBS cycle to recommend a final version of the Defense Guidance to the secretary. After considering the DRB recommendations, the secretary issued the Guidance to the services.

With the support of their headquarters staffs, the service secretaries and chiefs implemented the Defense Guidance through documents known as Program Objective Memoranda (POMs). Before the Reagan administration, the services were free to draft program documents without further review until they were forwarded to OSD in July. In 1985, however, Secretary Weinberger altered the process so that the Joint Chiefs and the theater commanders could review preliminary service POMs in May when they were delivered to OSD.[4] In June, OSD analysts, working with comments from the Joint Chiefs and the theater commanders, negotiated with the service headquarters staffs when, and if, there were disagreements over the POM numbers. OSD could try, for example, to pressure a service to shift planned funding from one program to another if OSD analysts believed that the service POM did not conform to the Defense Guidance. Throughout June negotiations between OSD and service headquarters staffs pared the number of POM issues to a minimum. The Defense Resources Board reviewed the POMs in August and the services were then allowed one final appeal before the Defense secretary made his judgment.

OSD review of Program Objective Memoranda was not entirely analytical. Organizational, doctrinal, and personal interests frequently came into play. They still do. The programming process is characterized by bargaining and posturing within each service headquarters and then between each headquarters and the OSD staff. Bargaining is necessary because the cost of all specific programs (research and development, training, acquisition, and personnel), which the service staffs would like to support, is greater than the funds available to support them. The relative scarcity of funds forces programmers to become politicians.

The service secretaries became an integral part of defense programming through participation both in the development of the Defense Guidance and in the adjudication process of the Defense Resources Board. Concerned also with the separation of the programming process from the acquisition process, Weinberger and Carlucci ensured that membership on the Defense Resources Board and on the Defense Systems Acquisition Review Council overlapped. Although Weinberger tied the programming and acquisition committees together, he kept real control for himself and his chief deputy. However, his decision to rely on the DRB as a major initiation and review body in the PPBS process enhanced the influence of the Navy secretary both at the DOD level and—more importantly—within the Navy.

Secretary of the Navy John F. Lehman, Jr., eagerly grasped and used this new influence. The most aggressive and organizationally perceptive Navy secretary since James Forrestal, Lehman set out to guide and shape the Navy after his appointment in 1981. He understood two things: the

Secretary of the Navy John F. Lehman, Jr., advocate of recommissioning the World War II *Iowa*-class battleships, on board *New Jersey* (BB-62).

primary activity of OPNAV was programming, and the major programming decisions were reached through a process of bargaining, review, and ratification by several layers of committees. The first committee level was the Program Development Review Committee, made up of rear admirals representing the CNO's major deputies and chaired by the Director of the General Planning and Programming Division (OP-90) within OP-090. The next level was the Program Review Committee, chaired by the Director of Navy Program Planning (OP-090). Capping the review process was the CNO Executive Board, chaired by the Vice Chief of Naval Operations and composed of the Chief of Naval Material, the Commandant of the Marine Corps, and the DCNOs. Most programming decisions were affirmed in the first two committees. The CNO could review those decisions, but he could not easily challenge them because his senior deputies were present or represented at each level of review and were accustomed to justifying their programs with analysis and argument. Secretary Lehman created the Navy Program Strategy Board, which he chaired, at a level above the CNO Executive Board, and he used the new board as part of his effort to take control of the programming process.

Like Secretary of Defense Weinberger, Lehman faced the problem of how to tie together a decentralized system so as to balance the initiative of subordinates with overall policy direction. As he noted in his memoirs, "We wanted to decentralize decision-making and delegate authority to the lowest appropriate level, but then to hold people accountable by name."[5] Lehman wanted to overcome the factions in the Navy and control the policy-making, or programming, process in OPNAV. To do that, he ignored the traditional separation of the secretary's acquisition authority and the CNO's programmatic duties. Lehman made his office not only the center of Navy programming but also the center of general Navy policy. He appropriated CNO Hayward's aggressive strategic concept and gave it widespread publicity as the Maritime Strategy. He also tapped the small but influential Strategic Studies Group, which Hayward had established at the Naval War College, and encouraged the faculty of the Navy's Postgraduate School in Monterey, California, to offer courses on strategic issues. He used his public and political visibility to push for a 600-ship Navy, based on Hayward's concept of a force built around fifteen aircraft carrier battle groups, and pressured Weinberger to increase the Navy's budget.

Secretary Lehman understood that success in Congress and in OSD would add to his credibility and his influence within the Navy. Lehman realized that the nature of the legislative process had changed in the 1970s, eroding the seniority system and creating many centers of influence. Thus, his strategy toward Congress had two parts. He based his long-term approach on a need to build, among members of the House and Senate, a recognition of the Navy's importance and a knowledge of its programs. Lehman assumed that he and his subordinates in the Office of Legislative Affairs could build awareness, understanding, and ultimately support in Congress, but only if the secretary spoke for the Navy. Accordingly, all Navy testimony before congressional committees was checked against the secretary's annual posture statement and any deviations from the statement were rejected.

The second part of Lehman's congressional strategy included an annual ranking of programs. Each November the secretary began a process of presenting congressional appropriation and authorization committees with briefings and testimonials in support of about eight programs most important to the secretary and the CNO. Between the fall of one year and committee mark-up time in the next, the Navy's presentations did not vary, even if Congress appeared unwilling to support all the programs suggested by the Secretariat. The Office of

Legislative Affairs became the focal point in this process. It tracked changes in congressional support for Navy programs and screened program managers and senior Navy officers called to testify. Program managers in the systems commands who balked at the guidance of the Secretariat were not permitted to speak for the Navy.[6]

Lehman also promoted the Maritime Strategy as a means of gaining visibility for the Navy in Congress and in the Office of the Secretary of Defense. To OSD, Lehman argued that Navy programs were based on a military strategy that made optimal use of the resources that a nation like the United States could and would produce. To Congress, Lehman argued that Navy forces were effective across a wide range of conflicts and mobile enough to deploy to the scene of a conflict in time to deal with it. To gain support within the Navy, Lehman presented himself as the provider and defender of the 600-ship fleet and as the advocate of the only coherent service strategy. He appealed to the fleet and its support units by visiting ships and bases, "campaigning" among the operating forces as politicians work their constituents. Indeed, as Captain Donald Stoufer, a former member of Lehman's staff, observed, "Lehman's philosophy was . . . control belongs with the operators, not at the Pentagon."[7]

Using this philosophy as a shield, Lehman deliberately undercut the influence of OPNAV and the CNO. According to Stoufer, "Secretary Lehman created an atmosphere of antagonism, fear, loathing, hate—almost any emotion. . . . Lehman was the consummate bureaucrat and yet he was anti-bureaucratic."[8] His goal was to break down the "Washington syndrome," or the view of OPNAV programmers that "the guy in the fleet doesn't know anything about the Navy or how the Navy operates, and therefore he—the programmer—is going to sit there and design a program that supports his view of the Navy."[9] Lehman's tactic in dealing with OPNAV was to threaten action, almost any action. "That was his tactic against OPNAV—not *long* hours. He didn't play their game."[10] The secretary used his formal powers to the utmost, guiding the deliberations of selection boards and the assignments of flag officers, controlling the public relations and congressional affairs aspects of the Navy Department, driving the programming process, and capturing the symbolic leadership role once the province of the Chief of Naval Operations.

Secretary Lehman understood that the key to dominating a bureaucracy was to gain and keep the initiative in ideas and in action. He carefully chose civilian deputies who shared his ideas, and he understood just how much influence he and his assistant secretaries had. For example, he used the Navy comptroller (a subordinate directly under the secretary) to limit funding for Navy operations and to discipline officers who mismanaged or abused Navy accounts. Lehman's strategy was "to

Admiral James D. Watkins, Chief of Naval Operations, 1982–1986.

U.S. Navy Photo

integrate the uniformed staff of the chief of naval operations and the commandant of the marine corps with the staff of the secretary of the navy."[11] After CNO Hayward's departure in 1982, Lehman began holding a series of Navy Strategy Board "retreats," where the secretary could confront the new CNO, Admiral James D. Watkins, in a setting where the admiral could not draw on the help of the OPNAV staff. As Lehman pointed out, the retreats in Boston, Virginia, broke down "the institutional barrier between the uniformed navy and marine corps and between them and the civilian leadership."[12] What he did not say was that he purposefully wanted to break down those barriers because they were a source of influence for the Chief of Naval Operations—if only because they kept "outsiders" (like Lehman) from setting the CNO's agenda.

The relationship between the secretary and his chiefs was rumored to have been difficult. It could not have been otherwise. Every strong Secretary of the Navy, from Josephus Daniels in the First World War to Forrestal at the close of the Second World War, has clashed with senior Navy officers, though not always with the CNO. By law, the secretary is responsible for the administration of the Navy Department. The CNO is his primary military assistant to whom the secretary usually delegates great authority. But John Lehman, like Forrestal, was anything but "normal" as a Navy secretary. Lehman's office—and sometimes the secretary personally—intervened in naval operations, planning, and acquisition to an unprecedented degree for peacetime. Lehman's audacity and brashness worked to keep the OPNAV bureaucracy off balance. His actions were unsettling and unusual, and his opponents claimed that they were detrimental to officer morale and bordered on the unethical. Many Navy officers clearly distrusted the secretary, but they could not openly resist him so long as he maintained the support of Weinberger and President Ronald Reagan and succeeded in pushing Navy budgets and authorizations through Congress.

With Lehman's concurrence, Admiral Watkins altered OPNAV's organization. After reviewing the studies and analysis activities in and sponsored by the office of the Director of Navy Program Planning, Watkins shifted certain functions assigned to branches in OP-090 to other organizations. He argued that the increased influence of the Director of Naval Warfare (OP-095) made the warfare task analysis function in OP-090 redundant. Watkins also transferred some of the responsibilities of the systems analysts in OP-090 to the DCNO for Plans, Policy, and Operations (OP-06), completing a process begun some years before. At the same time the new CNO established the Program Resource Appraisal Division (OP-91) that served as a "highly responsive action-oriented team able to take on key program issues on a timely basis."[13] At Lehman's insistence, VCNO Admiral William N. Small eliminated the Systems Analysis Division (OP-96) in March 1983 transferring its functions to the new OP-91.[14] In May, Watkins abolished the Long Range Planning Group (OP-00X) and moved its personnel into the CNO Executive Panel support staff (OP-00K).

While Watkins reorganized the OPNAV staff, Lehman instituted his own reforms. He transferred the control of the Center for Naval Analyses from OP-090 to the office of the Assistant Secretary of the Navy for Research, Engineering and Systems. Lehman's goal was to bring strategic analysis and planning under his control. He was openly hostile to systems analysts, whom he believed detracted from the work of Navy line managers. At the same time, however, he could not keep Navy officers from working on the Maritime Strategy, which he had embraced and championed. Accordingly, Watkins's Executive Panel began sponsoring an annual strategic planning conference, attended by the Navy's senior flag officers for the first time in September 1985.[15]

In his memoirs, Secretary Lehman discussed his and Watkin's efforts to modify the weapons acquisition process within the Navy. Lehman argued that the acquisition process was too centralized: "A single centralized procurement bureaucracy called the Navy Materiel

DN-ST-87-02289 U.S. Navy

Admiral Watkins (*left*), and Vice Admiral Nils R. Thunman, Deputy Chief of Naval Operations for Submarine Warfare, visit the control room of nuclear-powered attack submarine *Trepang* (SSN–674), July 1985.

Command reported to the chief of naval operations through his staff. . . . [A]ll the procurement and business organizations were under the total domination of the headquarters staff of the chief of naval operations, the OPNAV staff."[16] Lehman's assessment was not entirely correct. OPNAV, after all, was not really under the control of the CNO. Lehman himself admitted that the DCNOs for submarine, surface, and air warfare "controlled the project managers through some ninety 'commissars,' called 'project coordinators.' . . . Since. . . . virtually all project managers were unrestricted line . . . officers who hoped to get good assignments back with the fleet, they danced to the tune of the [DCNOs]."[17]

To break the deputy chiefs' power over project managers in the Navy's major acquisition commands, such as the Naval Sea Systems and Naval Air Systems commands, Lehman and Watkins changed the way financial deputies in the project offices were evaluated. They gave authority to write the fitness reports for such officers to the systems command comptrollers, who reported to the Assistant Secretary of the Navy for Financial Management (the Navy comptroller), removing the program managers, in whose offices the financial deputy worked, from the chain of command.[18] Watkins also gave the Director of Naval Warfare the authority to sponsor acquisition programs, a power which the deputy chiefs had almost totally monopolized.[19] And in the spring of 1985 Secretary Lehman abolished the Naval Material Command. As he explained in his memoirs:

> [W]e changed the reporting authority to have the commander of each of the systems commands report directly to the secretary of the navy and, on a parallel line, to the chief of naval operations for informational purposes. I had direct through lines put on my telephone to each of the systems commanders, and we talked back and forth almost daily.[20]

The talk was mostly one way.

Because "the blue suiters simply would not recognize any authority but the chief of naval operations," Lehman developed other means to increase or apply the influence of his office over acquisition and development.[21] He forced program managers in the Naval Sea Systems and Naval Air Systems commands to submit all requests for engineering change proposals to special review boards in each systems command. Contractors often requested such proposals to cover the increased cost of modifying a design at the government's request, hence raising the systems' costs. Ideally, such change proposals were used only as a last resort, when an unforeseen and unplanned design change had to be made. In fact, engineering change proposals were an "out" for program managers—a loophole that allowed (and some said encouraged) sloppy design practices. Lehman made all Navy program managers run requests for engineering changes through special screening boards, and if they passed that hurdle, through the CNO, and then finally to Lehman himself.

Lehman also required the major Navy buying commands (Naval Sea Systems and Naval Air Systems) to impose competition and fixed price contracts on the development and acquisition process. Using the legal authority vested in his office by Title 10 of the U.S. Code, he gave the Navy Secretariat greater influence over Navy procurement, research and development, and the Navy's relationship with major civilian contractors. Former Secretary Forrestal had done the same sort of thing in 1945 and 1946.

Yet Lehman, like Forrestal, traded benefits for increased influence within the Navy. The secretary was an effective advocate for Navy programs within the Defense Department and to Congress. Much of the Reagan administration's military build-up was in fact a Navy build-up. Even within the Navy, Lehman gained support by attacking established procedures or influential officers. In early 1982, for example, Lehman finally had enough congressional support to relieve Admiral Rickover as the Director of the Naval Nuclear Propulsion Program. Executive Order 12344 of 1 February 1982 limited the new director's term

DN-SN-86-10017 U.S. Navy

Secretary of the Navy John Lehman, with Virginia Senator John Warner looking on, congratulates Admiral Carlisle A. H. Trost, on the latter's appointment as Chief of Naval Operations at the U.S. Naval Academy, 30 June 1986.

to eight years and ordered him to report directly to the CNO. He also supported Watkins when the latter (like Hayward earlier) sought to control his own senior deputies. Indeed, because of the Navy secretary's influence over procurement, Lehman could work *around* the deputy chiefs, as he in fact did. Lehman was effective within the Navy because he offered both the carrot and the stick. It was difficult for senior officers to resist him, even if they wanted to.

In the congressional debates over defense reform, for example, Lehman took the same position that Arleigh Burke, as a captain, had expressed in 1949: the nation was protected from poor military advice and inordinate military influence by separate, coequal services, linked only loosely at the level of the Joint Chiefs of Staff. As Navy secretary, Lehman took the lead in opposing what became the Department of Defense Reorganization Act of 1986. Although he was not able to block the legislation, he gained influence within his service by arguing forcefully against strengthening the authority of the Chairman of the JCS.[22]

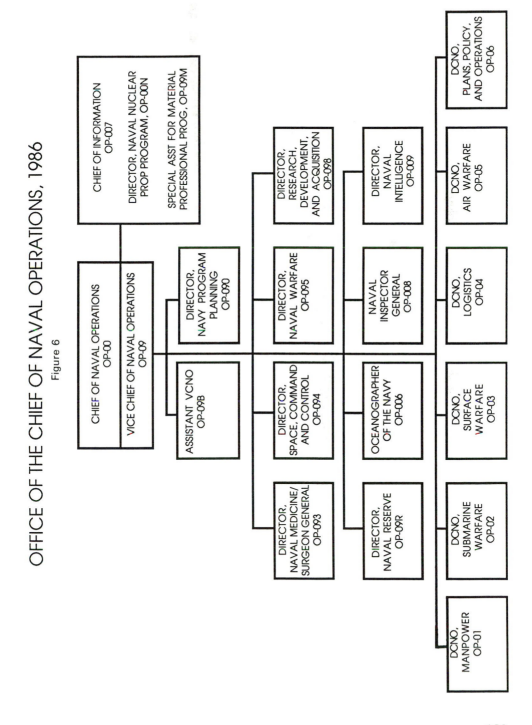

OFFICE OF THE CHIEF OF NAVAL OPERATIONS, 1986

Figure 6

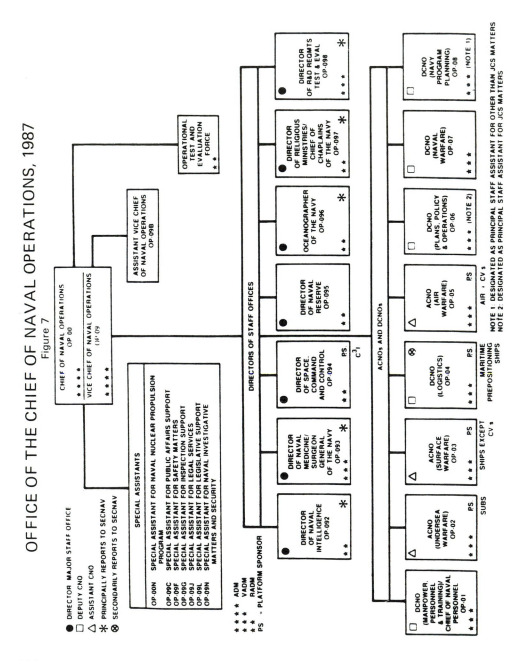

OFFICE OF THE CHIEF OF NAVAL OPERATIONS, 1987

Figure 7

Watkins's successor, Admiral Carlisle A. H. Trost used the reorganization act to strengthen his office. Section 5036 of the new law limited OPNAV to five Deputy Chiefs of Naval Operations; Section 5037 authorized no more than three assistant chiefs.[23] However, in 1986 there were six deputy chiefs. (See Figure 6.) Moreover, four of the directors who reported through the Vice Chief of Naval Operations could be considered assistant chiefs: Navy Program Planning (OP-090), Space, Command and Control (OP-094), Naval Warfare (OP-095), and Research, Development, and Acquisition (OP-098). Trost made the warfare area deputies *assistant* chiefs and the major directors *deputy* chiefs. The four new DCNOs became Manpower, Personnel, and Training (OP-01); Logistics (OP-04); Plans, Policy, and Operations (OP-06); Naval Warfare (OP-07); and Navy Program Planning (OP-08). The new ACNOs were Undersea Warfare (OP-02), Surface Warfare (OP-03), and Air Warfare (OP-05). This was a drastic shift away from the platform focus of OPNAV and back to the functional focus the organization had after the Second World War. (See Figure 7.) It was also a sign that the new CNO intended to shield his office from further encroachment by future Navy secretaries.

9

Conclusion

At the end of the Second World War, the Chief of Naval Operations was in fact the senior commanding officer in the United States Navy. After 1946, however, the *command* authority of the CNO was steadily reduced primarily through acts of Congress, which created and later strengthened the Department of Defense and made unified and specified field commanders the real commanders of deployed forces. After 1958 the CNO's operational command authority was based solely on his personality and the respect given the office. The 1986 DOD Reorganization Act added to the process begun in 1946. The difference was that it also increased the authority of the JCS chairman, perhaps better balancing the powers of civilian and military defense leaders.

Since the Second World War, the Office of the Chief of Naval Operations has also lost administrative authority. The Defense Cataloging and Standardization Act of 1953 and McNamara's imposition of the Planning, Programming, and Budgeting System in 1961 have reduced OPNAV's control over the shape and support of the Navy. Throughout the 1960s, for example, OPNAV's structure came to mirror that of the Office of the Secretary of Defense, and OPNAV's primary function became, like OSD's, programming. The functions once delegated to the Navy—planning, logistics, procurement—were shifted to joint (JCS) or civilian (DOD) agencies.

The pressures of integrating new technology into the fleet robbed post-World War II CNOs of initiative, even within OPNAV. Technology has moved ahead almost faster than the Navy has been able to move itself, and with each technological jump, OPNAV has responded by vesting a new piece of the Navy with a place at the programming table, so that the new technology could make a claim for resources. The process began in 1921, when the Navy accepted the argument that a new technology—aviation—needed special protection because its promise, not *then* clear, would never *become* clear unless it were given special protection. In the 1950s Rickover used a variation of this theme to develop a bureau-within-a-bureau to protect the nuclear power program. The creation of the platform sponsors (OPs 02, 03, 05) in 1971 wrested even more power from the CNO.

Admiral Rickover's success reveals the problem CNOs face as they try to affirm their own authority. Rickover argued persuasively that nuclear accidents would destroy Navy and civilian nuclear power programs. Hence, centralized, rigid control had to be maintained over those programs in order to keep them as accident-free as possible. Rigid control was impossible, however, where authority and responsibility were dispersed, and the logical place to focus authority and responsibility was on the experts in the new technology. This argument was hard to deny, and one of its implications was that the power of the CNO would be steadily reduced unless OPNAV itself maintained control over technological development. CNOs had tried giving development DCNO status and then a position as a principal deputy to the vice chief, but there was no easy way for OPNAV to put all new technology under one office. The number of technological developments needing support outgrew the available financial resources. The development of the Polaris-armed, nuclear submarine system, for example, was financed by cutting or killing other Navy programs, including a long-range cruise missile and a jet-powered, long-range seaplane. The struggle for scarce resources was so difficult for the Navy because, after Burke's tenure, the Chief of Naval Operations gradually lost control of the process by which force structure decisions were made. By the late 1960s platform, mission, and program sponsors wanted the CNO's authority. If they could get it without surrendering any of their own power in return, and they often could, then they did so. The CNO could not command the programming process if he lacked the skills of an organizational politician. Indeed, his initiatives, voiced within the JCS at the very beginning of the PPBS cycle, were not even cost-constrained, and hence had little impact on what happened within his own service.

As Admiral Zumwalt found in the early 1970s, setting up a systems analysis office in OPNAV did not solve the problem. The Navy needed a doctrine around which to plan, so that "the true determinants of service interest and service emphasis," instead of being "concealed within the individual service organizations," would be out in the open.[1] CNOs Hayward and Watkins attempted to define a planning doctrine with the Maritime Strategy, but found they could not impose this strategic concept on the systems commands. Although opinions about the tenure of Secretary Lehman are colored by reactions to his often abrasive and clearly ambitious personality, it seems clear from his tenure that only the secretary himself, given his statutory authority, can create an atmosphere in which OPNAV can persuade the systems commands to embrace something like the Maritime Strategy. In effect, the CNO has lost so much administrative authority within the Navy that only the secretary has the capability of pulling OPNAV, the systems commands, and the fleet together.

Yet the decline of the CNO's administrative authority has not reduced his work load. As former CNO David McDonald put it, "I came nearer running the Navy when I was aide to Dan Kimball and he was Under

Secretary than I did when I was CNO. . . . When I was CNO, I often felt that I had no more authority than a Lieutenant Commander."[2] The reason is clear: McDonald was subject to the initiatives of others, such as the Secretary of Defense, and he was not on close-enough personal terms with Robert McNamara to affect the secretary's thinking. The CNO was a relatively weak executive, often reactive and dependent, and lacking the authority and the staff organization to control the bureaus and, later, the systems commands. By the time Zumwalt became CNO, OPNAV resembled the headquarters of many federal agencies: sensitive to congressional scrutiny, anxious to avoid close and clear direction by both Congress and the executive branch, and characterized by fragmented authority that balked at central direction and contributed to the formation of alliances between headquarters staff and quasi-independent field units. In this system, the CNO had to work more hours and put in greater effort not only to meet growing OSD demands, but also to keep track of what his subordinates were doing.

This does not mean CNOs after 1961 were powerless. Herbert Kaufman pointed out in his studies of federal bureaucracies that public officials with limited authority could be important to maintaining organizational solidarity, setting a certain style of leadership and training new generations of organizational leaders, building up their organizations' public images, cultivating congressional support, and stimulating new approaches to continuing problems and responsibilities.[3] Since 1958 the CNOs have had to struggle to avoid becoming like the senior officials in most civilian agencies. Even under a strong secretary like John Lehman, however, CNOs have found problems worthy of their talents and energy. Admiral Hayward, for example, sought to eliminate drug abuse as a serious Navy problem. His successor, Admiral Watkins, apparently played an important role in President Reagan's decision to endorse the Strategic Defense Initiative concept.

This study returns to the argument of Vincent Davis: that Navy officers became politically influential to gain autonomy and independence for themselves and for their service (or branch of the service). They were always uneasy with the concept of firm central management and the idea that the major duties of a service chief were as much political as military. This tradition of suspicion toward military officers with political skills and ambitions prevented Navy officers from accomplishing what Secretary Lehman did in the 1980s. John Lehman recognized that the CNO—*because* he was a Navy officer—might have problems learning to use effectively the kind of authority required to gain control over Navy programming, planning, and acquisition. CNOs had to become clever bureaucrats with a sense of organizational integrity. Because their concept of integrity was operational instead of bureaucratic, they were limited in what they thought they could do and in what they allowed themselves to think and do. They were trained and prepared for military command, but the CNO's job is *not* a position of military command—it is a position of organizational leadership, requiring political and social skills that are not best learned in an operational setting.

In his classic study of General Motors, Peter Drucker argued that "the most important problem of modern society" was "the problem of responsibility, of authority, and of competence of the large organization."[4] The Navy would agree with this assessment. Officers are trained to be responsible, competent, and capable of exercising authority. That is precisely why the Chief of Naval Operations must have strong operational command credentials. It is also one reason why some postwar CNOs had greater influence than others. Admiral Sherman, for example, had been deputy chief of staff to Fleet Admiral Nimitz during the war; Admiral Carney had served as Admiral William F. Halsey's chief of staff; Admiral Burke was the wartime chief of staff to then Vice Admiral Marc A. Mitscher; and Admiral Anderson was plans officer for Vice Admiral John Towers, Nimitz's deputy in the Pacific. Later CNOs, too young to have achieved significant command experience, or any experience, in the Second World War had different credentials. Even Admiral Moorer, who did have command experience during the war, gained additional visibility and credibility as head of CNO Burke's Long Range Objectives Group (OP-93). Zumwalt learned his political skills as aide to Secretary of the Navy Paul Nitze and as the first head of the Systems Analysis Division (OP-96) in OPNAV. Experience in OPNAV, either as director of a major staff organization or as the vice chief (as Watkins was), became the prerequisites for the prospective CNO. But the position still required a reputation for having significant operational leadership.

In an organization such as the Navy, where officers are suspicious of organizational skills unless they are paired with operational competence, the CNO must project the image of being a skilled—and even daring—operator. Subordinates will not grant him legitimacy if he lacks that image. When Drucker studied General Motors, he found that it, like the Navy, was a decentralized organization with autonomous divisions. He also found that to maintain a successful organization (that is, to produce both products and quality leaders, and to give employees a sense that their work was worthwhile), General Motors needed the market with its consumer audience. Sales indicated the level of performance of both central and divisional managers. Moreover, sales figures were public. Given the powers of GM managers, it was clear that the blame for poor sales performance was theirs alone. The Navy's equivalent of sales was, and still is, operations, not positions of programming and budgeting.

The Navy, like all effective modern military organizations, is an extraordinary bureaucracy, although some naval personnel protest that it is not a bureaucracy at all. They do so because naval service implies a commitment not usually associated with the term bureaucracy. At the operational level, Navy personnel routinely do extraordinary things such as launching and recovering high-speed, large jet aircraft from carrier decks and taking large submarines under the north polar icecap. They perform these often dangerous, always difficult, tasks only because they belong to an organization that encourages responsibility, competence, and initiative. According to a recently published study of aircraft carrier operations, orthodox "organizational theory would characterize aircraft carrier operations as confusing and inefficient, especially for an organization with a strong and steep, formal management hierarchy. . . . However, the resulting redundancy and flexibility are, in fact, remarkably efficient in terms of making the best use of space-limited personnel."[5] Hence, the ethics of operations are pragmatic, problem-focused, and mutual. People solve problems by working together, driven by the need to achieve results. Navy personnel in operations feel obliged to work this way.

Consequently, officers with operational skills are often ill at ease when this sense of shared obligation is absent or weak. Their discomfort is as much ethical as behavioral, or social. They do not find, in organizations like OPNAV, an ethical atmosphere that compares to that in the fleet. They often try to impose their fleet experiences on their OPNAV duties. The result is usually what students of organizations call "goal displacement": not knowing for sure what is expected or what is effective, officers focus their energies on tasks that they can master and on projects that they can control. As a result, for example, a letter is often drafted six or seven times, or an individual problem or topic is studied to death. Officers in OPNAV or the systems commands, who would never waste time on petty issues while serving in the fleet, argue over whose name should appear first at the bottom of a jointly drafted letter.

OPNAV is a loose confederation, not an operational organization. In the fleet, getting the job done efficiently and effectively has priority. In OPNAV, measures of performance differ. For programmers, the mark of success is placing an item in the Navy's Program Objectives Memorandum and multiyear defense plan. For policy specialists, success may mean influencing the Joint Staff. As a result, the various offices in OPNAV compete with one another, and often there is no logical connection between force and strategic planning and programming. Indeed, the very aggressiveness and focus on problem-solving that are rewarded in the fleet may make an officer vulnerable in OPNAV, where informal contacts and a perception of who has the real influence are the keys to success.

Furthermore, the functions once done exclusively within OPNAV (or in the fleet staffs) are now done by others, or jointly. The Secretary of Defense sets priorities; Congress can and does intervene in the procurement process as well as in policy areas once controlled by executive branch agencies. In the fleet, officers and enlisted personnel are forced to reorganize continually because of personnel rotations. Turnovers give individuals the chance to learn new skills and to switch associations, thereby offering a chance to perform and excel. This sense of learning and achieving is difficult to foster in OPNAV, because much of what happens within OPNAV is not under the control of the officers who run the organization. Under these circumstances it is surprising that OPNAV is as effective as it is.

* * *

Are the obstacles to successful leadership, which face any future Chief of Naval Operations, more than any capable senior naval officer can overcome? OPNAV's postwar history does not support an affirmative answer to that question. The evidence is strong that even after 1958, when the CNO was stripped of his operational command authority, the position continued to exert strong influence on both OPNAV and the Navy. To pose the question another way, Aside from the Second World War, when the CNO was also the Commander in Chief, did prewar CNOs have an easier task than their postwar counterparts? The answer is no. Prewar CNOs had to justify spending requests before Congress and to the President; the Navy's bureaus were largely independent of direct OPNAV control; and the CNO supported the U.S. Fleet but did not command it. Granted that there was no OSD and that OPNAV staffs were small, but the problems of leadership and coordination were no less strenuous than those of postwar CNOs.

Near the door to the office of the President of the Naval War College is a portrait of Rear Admiral William V. Pratt, former president of the college, Commander in Chief, U.S. Fleet, and Chief of Naval Operations (1930-1933). Despite his talents as a commander and leader, Pratt was disliked by many of his professional contemporaries. Although now respected by naval historians, Pratt nevertheless retired as Chief of Naval Operations under a cloud, criticized by many of his peers for having apparently allowed the strength of the Navy to be reduced to a dangerously low level. In opposition to most senior Navy officers, Pratt had supported the Washington Naval Conference agreements of 1921, and as a senior official at the London Conference in 1930, he had worked out a compromise with the Royal Navy that most of his contemporaries regarded as harmful to the interests of the U.S. Navy. What Pratt actually did, however, was smooth over a serious rift between the two navies and, in doing so, laid the foundation for Anglo-American naval cooperation in the Second World War. Having no control over President Hoover's decision to decrease the Navy budget, Pratt was forced to economize and to search for unorthodox ways to stretch the Navy's military potential.[6]

Pratt's troubles would sound familiar to any contemporary CNO: senior civilians distrusted him; he faced a hostile Congress and a critical press; he never had money to modernize the fleet or to pay for the required numbers of personnel; he had to compete with another service for resources; and the "barons" within his own service continually disputed his authority. These conditions limited Pratt's accomplishments. What a CNO can do is clearly affected then by the conditions under which he serves. At the same time, however, he can affect those conditions both directly, through his own leadership, and indirectly, through relations with others who can then act in ways which support him. Admiral Zumwalt was conscious of this fact when he deliberately established policies that drew on the energy and intelligence of younger, dedicated officers. Admiral Hayward was thinking in these terms when he started the process that led to what is now called the Maritime Strategy. Admiral Burke is a prime example of effective leadership even though his views on defense organization were at odds with those of President Eisenhower.

The point is, a creative Chief of Naval Operations may be able to turn the pressures that can limit his effectiveness into an advantage for both himself and the Navy. The CNO position carries great prestige, visibility (both within the Navy and in the public eye), and potential influence. The officer holding the position gains access to OPNAV, Congress, the Joint Chiefs, and even the White House. There is no guarantee that a CNO will turn such access into real influence, but the opportunity for him to do so exists.

Appendixes

A. Secretaries of the Navy
1946-1986

James V. Forrestal	May 1944–September 1947
John L. Sullivan	September 1947–May 1949
Francis P. Matthews	May 1949–July 1951
Dan A. Kimball	July 1951–January 1953
Robert B. Anderson	February 1953–May 1954
Charles S. Thomas	May 1954–March 1957
Thomas S. Gates, Jr.	April 1957–June 1959
William B. Franke	June 1959–January 1961
John B. Connally, Jr.	January 1961–December 1961
Fred H. Korth	January 1962–November 1963
Paul H. Nitze	November 1963–June 1967
Paul R. Ignatius	September 1967–January 1969
John H. Chafee	January 1969–May 1972
John W. Warner	May 1972–April 1974
J. William Mittendorf II	June 1974–January 1977
W. Graham Claytor, Jr.	February 1977–August 1979
Edward Hidalgo	October 1979–January 1981
John F. Lehman, Jr.	February 1981–April 1987

B. Chiefs of Naval Operations
1946-1986

Fleet Admiral Chester W. Nimitz	December 1945–December 1947
Admiral Louis E. Denfeld	December 1947–November 1949
Admiral Forrest P. Sherman	November 1949–July 1951
Admiral William M. Fechteler	August 1951–August 1953
Admiral Robert B. Carney	August 1953–August 1955
Admiral Arleigh A. Burke	August 1955–August 1961
Admiral George W. Anderson, Jr	August 1961–August 1963
Admiral David L. McDonald	August 1963–August 1967
Admiral Thomas H. Moorer	August 1967–July 1970
Admiral Elmo R. Zumwalt, Jr.	July 1970–July 1974
Admiral James L. Holloway III	July 1974–July 1978
Admiral Thomas B. Hayward	July 1978–June 1982
Admiral James D. Watkins	June 1982–June 1986
Admiral Carlisle A. H. Trost	June 1986–

Abbreviations

ACNO	Assistant Chief of Naval Operations
BUAER	Bureau of Aeronautics
BUSHIPS	Bureau of Ships
BUWEPS	Bureau of Weapons
CIA	Central Intelligence Agency
CNO	Chief of Naval Operations
COMINCH	Commander in Chief, U.S. Fleet
DCNO	Deputy Chief of Naval Operations
DIA	Defense Intelligence Agency
DOD	Department of Defense
DRB	Defense Resources Board
DSARC	Defense Systems Acquisition Review Council
JAG	Judge Advocate General
JSTPS	Joint Strategic Target Planning Staff
NAVWAG	Naval Warfare Analysis Group
NSC	National Security Council
NWP	Naval Warfare Publication
OMB	Office of Management and Budget
OPA	Office of Program Assessment
OPNAV	Office of the Chief of Naval Operations
OSD	Office of the Secretary of Defense
POM	Program Objective Memorandum
PPBS	Planning, Programming, and Budgeting System
SAC	Strategic Air Command

Abbreviations

SALT	Strategic Arms Limitation Treaty
SCOROR	Secretary's Committee on Research on Reorganization
SECDEF	Secretary of Defense
SECNAV	Secretary of the Navy
SPO	Special Projects Office
SPP	Sponsor Program Proposal

Notes

The primary sources cited in this study are found in two Washington, D.C. locations. The Organization and OPNAV Resource Management Division (OP-09B2) of the Office of the Chief of Naval Operations in the Pentagon holds the OPNAV Historical Records, referred to as OP-09B2 Records in the notes. Other documents, including the author's collection, are held in the Operational Archives Branch of the Naval Historical Center. Short forms and full citations for this material are as follows:

> 00 File—Records of the Immediate Office of the CNO
> OP-23—Records of the Organizational Research and Policy Division
> OP-602—Records of the Plans, Policy, and Command Organization Branch, DCNO for Plans and Policy (OP-06) (unprocessed)
> Command File—Post 1 January 1946 Command File

1. Administration versus Command

1. Vincent Davis, *The Admirals Lobby* (Chapel Hill, NC, 1967), pp. 40-41.

2. Ibid., pp. 74-100; Thomas C. Hone, "Navy Air Leadership: Rear Admiral William A. Moffett as Chief of the Bureau of Aeronautics," in *Air Leadership*, ed. Wayne Thompson (Washington, 1986), pp. 83-118.

3. See Michael A. Palmer, *Origins of the Maritime Strategy: American Naval Strategy in the First Postwar Decade* (Washington, 1988).

4. Rufus F. Zogbaum, *From Sail to Saratoga* (Rome, n.d.), p. 465.

5. Hone, "Navy Air Leadership: Rear Admiral William A. Moffett," pp. 83-118.

6. See Richard G. Hewlett and Francis Duncan, *Nuclear Navy* (Chicago, 1974).

7. General Board Study No. 446 (1933-39), "Organization of the Navy Department," 24 Jan 1934. Microfilm copy held by Operational Archives.

8. Ibid.

9. Naval Air Systems Command, *United States Naval Aviation, 1910-1970*, (Washington, 1970), p. 35. Italics added.

10. Robert Greenhalgh Albion and Robert Howe Connery, *Forrestal and the Navy* (New York, 1962), pp. 227-28.

11. Ibid., pp. 231-33, 238-39.

12. Ibid., pp. 234-36.

13. Ibid., pp. 237-38.

14. Ibid., p. 240.

15. Vincent Davis, *Postwar Defense Policy and the U.S. Navy, 1943-1946* (Chapel Hill, NC, 1967), p. 37. The Woodrum Committee (Select Committee on Post-War Military Policy) hearings are described on pp. 54-65.

16. Ibid., p. 66.

17. Ibid., pp. 204-205.

18. Ibid., p. 203.

19. Ibid., pp. 126-27
20. Ibid., p. 149.
21. Ibid., p. 238.
22. Ibid., p. 15.

2. Postwar Challenges

1. Norman Friedman, *The Postwar Naval Revolution* (Annapolis, MD, 1986), Chap. 1.

2. John T. Greenwood, "The Emergence of the Postwar Strategic Air Force, 1945-1953," in *Air Power and Warfare,* Proceedings of the 8th Military History Symposium, U.S. Air Force Academy, eds. Alfred F. Hurley and Robert C. Ehrhart (Washington, 1979), pp. 218-21.

3. Friedman, *The Postwar Naval Revolution*, p. 9.

4. Greenwood, "The Emergence of the Postwar Strategic Air Force, 1945-1953." See also David A. Rosenberg, "American Postwar Air Doctrine and Organization: The Navy Experience," in *Air Power and Warfare*, pp. 245-78.

5. See Senate Committee on Naval Affairs, *Unification of the War and Navy Departments and Postwar Organization for National Security* (Ferdinand Eberstadt Report), 79th Cong., 1st sess., 12 Oct 1945.

6. Davis, *Postwar Defense Policy*, p. 236.

7. Joint Committee on the Investigation of the Pearl Harbor Attack, *Investigation of the Pearl Harbor Attack: Report*, 79th Cong., 2d sess., 1946, S. Doc. 244; see also *Investigation of the Pearl Harbor Attack: Hearings*, 39 vols., 79th Cong., 2d sess., 1946; and Gordon Prange, *At Dawn We Slept* (New York, 1981).

8. "Decisions Leading to the Establishment of Unified Commands," JCS, Post-1 Jan 1946 Command File (hereafter Command File).

9. Greenwood, "The Emergence of the Postwar Strategic Air Force, 1945-1953," p. 227.

10. Memo, Carney to Nimitz, 25 Nov 1946, subj: Merger Discussions, file 31 (Memos, CNO, Personal, 1942-47), box 2, Records of the Immediate Office of the CNO (hereafter 00 File).

11. Hone, "Navy Air Leadership: Rear Admiral William A. Moffett," pp. 83-118.

12. Davis, *Postwar Defense Policy*, pp. 124-25.

13. Department of the Navy, *United States Navy Regulations, 1920*, Reprint (Washington, 1941), sec. 5.

14. Palmer, *Origins of the Maritime Strategy*, chap. 3.

15. Rosenberg, "American Postwar Air Doctrine and Organization," p. 11.

16. Historical Division, Joint Secretariat, Joint Chiefs of Staff, *A Concise History of the Organization of the Joint Chiefs of Staff, 1942-1978* (Washington, 1979), p. 17.

17. Robert Frank Futrell, *Ideas, Concepts, Doctrine: A History of Basic Thinking in the United States Air Force, 1907-1964* (Maxwell AFB, AL, 1971), p. 115.

18. Ibid., p. 117.

19. Ibid., p. 116.

20. Steven L. Rearden, *History of the Office of the Secretary of Defense*, vol. 1, *The Formative Years, 1947-1950* (Washington, 1984), p. 316.

21. Ibid., pp. 395-96; see also Futrell, *Ideas, Concepts, Doctrine*, pp. 99-100.

22. Paolo E. Coletta, "Louis Emil Denfeld," in *The Chiefs of Naval Operations*, ed. Robert William Love, Jr. (Annapolis, MD, 1980), pp. 196-97.

23. Walter Millis, ed., with the collaboration of E. F. Duffield, *The Forrestal Diaries* (New York, 1951), pp. 476-77.

24. Robert H. Connery, *The Navy and the Industrial Mobilization in World War II* (Princeton, 1951), p. 440.

25. Rosenberg, "American Postwar Air Doctrine and Organization," p. 256.

26. See Robert Greenhalgh Albion and Samuel H. P. Read, Jr., *The Navy at Sea and Ashore* (Washington, 1947).

27. Coletta, "Louis Emil Denfeld," p. 197.

28. Ibid., p. 198.

29. Memo, Burke to Denfeld, 3 Mar 1949, subj: Comments on "The National Security Organization" by the Commission on Organization of the Executive Branch of the Government, A20/4 National Security Organization folder, Records of the Organizational Research and Policy Division (hereafter OP-23 File).

30. Memo, Burke to Carney, 5 Aug 1949, subj: Comptroller of the Navy, A1/EM-3/4, OP-23 File.

31. Memo, Burke to Chairman, General Board of the Navy, 7 Sep 1949, subj: Study of the Applicability of the General Staff System to the Navy, A1/EM-3/4, OP-23 File.

32. Memo, Carney to Chairman, General Board of the Navy, 4 Aug 1949, subj: Study of the General Staff System Applicability to the Navy, folder 70, box 5, Records of the Plans, Policy, and Command Organization Branch (unprocessed) (hereafter OP-602 File).

33. Memo, "Trends in Unification," 16 Oct 1949, p. 1, A1/EM-3/4, OP-23 File.

34. Ibid.

35. U.S. Statutes, *National Security Act Amendments of 1949*, Public Law 216, vol. 63, pt. 1 (10 Aug 1949), pp. 578-90; see also Futrell, *Ideas, Concepts, Doctrine*, pp. 129-34, 136.

36. Memo, "Trends in Unification," 16 Oct 1949, p. 13, A1/EM-3/4, OP-23 File.

37. Ibid., p. 14.

38. Rosenberg, "American Postwar Air Doctrine and Organization," p. 263.

39. Ibid., pp. 261-62.

40. Friedman, *The Postwar Naval Revolution*, p. 9.

3. The Eisenhower Years

1. The Rockefeller Committee was chaired by Nelson Rockefeller; other members were General of the Army Omar N. Bradley; Vannevar Bush, president of the Carnegie Institution; Milton Eisenhower, president of then-Pennsylvania State College; Arthur Flemming; Robert Lovett, former Secretary of Defense; and David Sarnoff, head of RCA.

2. Senate Committee on Armed Services, *Department of Defense Organization: Report of the Rockefeller Committee*, 83rd Cong., 1st sess., 1953, p. 1.

3. Ibid., pp. 2-3, 5, 9, 11, 12.

4. *Message from the President of the United States, Reorganization Plan No. 6 of 1953, Relating to the Department of Defense*, 83rd Cong., 1st sess., 1953, H. Doc. 136, pp. 9-10.

5. Historical Division, Joint Secretariat, Joint Chiefs of Staff, *Chronology, Functions and Composition of the Joint Chiefs of Staff* (Washington, 1979), p. 209.

6. Ibid., p. 210.

7. Department of the Navy, *Report of the Committee on Organization of the Department of the Navy* (Thomas S. Gates Committee Report) (Washington, 1954), p. 34.

8. Ibid., pp. 34-35.

9. Ibid., pp. 41-44.

10. Paul R. Schratz, "Robert Bostwick Carney," in *The Chiefs of Naval Operations*, p. 248.

11. "Historical Perspectives in Long Range Planning in the Navy," draft, pt. 1: "The Planning Process in Overview, 1900-1978, for the Naval Research Advisory Committee, May 1979, p. vi-1, Author's collection.

12. Schratz, "Robert Bostwick Carney," p. 256.

13. Rosenberg, "Arleigh Albert Burke," p. 275.

14. Norman Friedman, *U.S. Naval Weapons* (Annapolis, MD, 1984), pp. 150-58.

15. Department of the Navy, "Report of the Board Convened by the Chief of Naval Operations to Study and Report Upon the Adequacy of the Bureau System of Organization" (R. E. Libby Board Report), ser 05754, 14 Mar 1956, p. iii, Command File.

16. Ibid., p. III-9.

17. Ibid., p. III-11.

18. Ibid., p. III-32.

19. Ibid., pp. I-1-2

20. Ibid., p. III-9

21. Rosenberg, "Arleigh Albert Burke," p. 279.

4. Burke: Shielding the Navy

1. John R. Wadleigh, "Thomas Sovereign Gates, Jr.," in *American Secretaries of the Navy*, vol. 2, ed. Paolo E. Coletta (Annapolis, MD, 1980), p. 883.

2. Memo for the Record, subj: Chronology—Reorganization Act of 1958, 30 Aug 1961, folder 33, 1958 Bills—DOD Reorganization, box 3, OP-602 File. For Eisenhower's views, see Stephen E. Ambrose, *Eisenhower*, vol. 2, *The President* (New York, 1984), p. 428.

3. Memo for the Record, 1 Jun 1961, subj: Appointment of Rep. Paul Kilday to Court of Military Appeals, folder 49, DOD Reorganization-1961, box 3, OP-602 File.

4. Rosenberg, "Arleigh Albert Burke," pp. 280-82.

5. Ibid., p. 302.

6. Ibid., p. 303.

7. Ibid., pp. 303-304.

8. Department of the Navy, "Staff Study on Organization of the Office of the Chief of Naval Operations" (A. L. Reed Study), 5430 OPNAV/OP-00, pp. 1-2, Aug 43-Dec 61 folder, OPNAV Historical Records, Organization and OPNAV Resource Management Division (OP-09B2), Pentagon (hereafter OP-09B2 Records).

9. Ibid., p. 2.

10. Ibid.

11. Ibid., p. 3.

12. Ibid., p. 5.

13. Ibid., p. 6.

14. Ibid., p. 7.

15. Department of the Navy, *Report of the Committee on Organization of the Department of the Navy* (Franke Board Report) (Washington, 1959), pp. 17-37, 56-58.

16. Wadleigh, "Thomas Sovereign Gates, Jr.," p. 888.

17. Memo, OPNAV Ad Hoc Committee to Review the Navy Department Organization to Burke, 25 Jul 1958, subj: Preliminary Report, p. 3, folder 70, box 3, OP-602 File.

18. Edwin B. Hooper, "Draft to Form the Basis of a Possible Study on Navy Department Reorganization," Navy Department Library, NHC.

19. Memo, Leverton to Burke, 19 Jun 1959, subj: Chief of Bureau of Weapons, folder 39, DOD Reorganization—1959, box 1, OP-602 File. The memo is unsigned, but it was apparently written on the same typewriter used for other memos prepared by Captain Joseph W. Leverton, and is stored with other papers written and signed by Leverton.

20. "ADM Hopwood's Three Fleet Concept for the Pacific," folder 12, CINCPACFLT-1948-DATE, box 3, OP-602 File.

21. Memo, Burke to OP-06, DCNO (Plans and Policy), OP-00 Memo 511-59, 2 Oct 1959, subj: Revised Joint Table of Distribution for CINCPAC Staff, folder C22, Command in the Pacific, vol. 1, OP-602 File.

22. Memos, unsigned, but probably meant for CNO Burke, 9 Apr 1959, subj: Dealing out of Channels; OPNAV Opinion, 6 Apr 1959, folder 39, box 1, OP-602 File. Both memos appear to have been written on Captain Leverton's typewriter.

23. Ltr, Burke to Schindler, 5 Oct 1959, subj: Organization of the Dept. of Defense, folder 39, box 1, OP-602 File.

24. "The Need for a Look at DOD Organization," OP-06D, ser 109P06D, 15 May 1961, folder 49, DOD Reorganization-1961, box 1, Organizational files, OP-602 File.

25. Ibid.

26. "Symington Committee Report to Senator Kennedy on Defense Reorganization—Brief of Legislative Versus Administrative Changes," folder 50, Monograph: DOD Reorganization, box 3, OP-602 File.

27. Knoll, Memo for the Record, "Meeting with Admiral Burke on 15 August," OP-06D, 16 Aug 1960, folder 41, DOD Reorganization, 1 Jan-30 Sep 1960, box 2, OP-602 File.

28. Ltr, Knoll to address list, 8 Aug 1960, subj: Following the Presidential Campaign, folder 41, box 2, OP-602 File.

29. Ltr, Andrew Hoyem, CO, USN&MCRTC, to Knoll, 19 Aug 1960, subj: Response to Knoll's Letter of 8 Aug, folder 41, box 2, OP-602 File.

30. "Reorganization of the Department of Defense: Philosophy and Counter-Philosophy," p. A-14, folder 45, JAG Studies on DOD Reorganization-1960, box 3, OP-602 File.

31. Ibid., p. A-15.

32. Memorandum to the File, 10 October 1960 meeting of CNO Burke and aides, 12 Oct 1960, para. 4, folder 49, box 1, OP-602 File.

33. Ibid., para. 15.

34. Memo, Acting Deputy Chief of Legislative Affairs, Navy Department, to SECNAV, CNO, and Commandant of the Marine Corps, 7 Dec 1960, subj: Report to Senator Kennedy from Committee on the Defense Establishment, Historical Evolution folder, box 1, OP-602 File.

35. A number of future CNOs and VCNOs served as Long Range Planning chiefs or heads of OP-96 (Systems Analysis), including Admirals Thomas H. Moorer, Elmo R. Zumwalt, Jr., and Horacio Rivero.

36. OASD (Comptroller), "Department of the Navy, Organization and Decision-Making Study," 3 Nov 1961, Executive Summary, p. 12, Historical Evolution folder, box 1, OP-602 File.

37. Ibid., p. 19.

38. Ibid., p. 13.

39. Ibid., p. 19.

40. Arnold R. Shapack, ed., *Proceedings Naval History Symposium*, U.S. Naval Academy 27-28 Apr 1973 (Annapolis, MD, 1973), p. 90.

41. Rosenberg, "Arleigh Albert Burke," p. 297.

42. OASD (Comptroller), "Department of the Navy, Organization and Decision-Making Study," Summary, pp. 46-47.

5. The McNamara Revolution

1. Rosenberg, "Arleigh Burke," p. 308.

2. Paul R. Schratz, "John B. Connally," in *American Secretaries of the Navy*, 2: 914.

3. Lawrence Korb, "George Whalen Anderson, Jr.," in *The Chiefs of Naval Operations*, pp. 321-32. Anderson's successor, Admiral David L. McDonald, avoided the TFX issue because he saw no way of convincing McNamara to drop his support for the plane. What finally killed the TFX as the aircraft for both the Air Force and the Navy was the Navy's revival, under the leadership of Vice Admiral Thomas F. Connally, DCNO (Air), of a different fighter concept, now represented by the combination of the F-14 and the Phoenix long-range, air-to-air missile. Floyd D. Kennedy, Jr., "David Lamar McDonald," in *The Chiefs of Naval Operations*, pp. 333-50. See also Friedman, *U.S. Naval Weapons*, pp. 177-78.

4. Department of the Navy, *Review of Management of the Department of the Navy*, study 1, vol. 2, *External Environmental Influences Study*, Study Director J. V. Smith (Washington, 1962), p. 39.

5. Ibid., Appendix G, "Statement of Asst. Secretary of Defense Charles J. Hitch Before the Military Operations Subcommittee of the House Committee on Government Operations," 25 Jul 1962, p. 184.

6. Ibid., p. 191.

7. [Smith], *External Environmental Influences Study*, 2: 40.

8. Ibid., p. 44.

9. Ibid., p. 47.

10. Department of the Navy, *Review of Management of the Department of the Navy*, study 2, vol. 1, *Planning, Programming, Budgeting, and Appraising Study*, Study Director H. A. Renken (Washington, 1962), p. 22.

11. Ibid., p. 23.

12. [Renken], *Planning, Programming, Budgeting, and Appraising Study*, 1: 3, 5.

13. Department of the Navy, *Review of Management of the Department of the Navy* (John H. Dillon Board Report) (Washington, 1962), p. 85.

14. Ibid., p. 86.

15. Ibid., p. 52.

16. Ibid., pp. 8, 102.

17. Ibid. See final pages of the Dillon Board Report.

18. Ibid., p. 12.

19. Charles K. Duncan, interview by John T. Mason, Jr., 1983, 3 vols., 3: 1269, U.S. Naval Institute (USNI) Oral History, Annapolis, MD (hereafter Duncan Oral History).

20. Dillon Board Report, p. 28.

21. Ibid., pp. 110-111.

22. Ibid., p. 9.

23. Schratz, "Fred Korth," in *American Secretaries of the Navy*, 2: 931.

24. Memo, The Need for a Look at DOD Organization," under cover ltr OP-06D, ser 109P06D, 15 May 1961, pt. 4, p. 5, folder 49, DOD Reorganization-1961, OP-602 File.

25. Department of the Navy, *Navy Organization Study* (Roy S. Benson Task Force Report) (Washington, 1966), p. A-1.

26. Memo, "Erosion of the Military Profession," n.d., p. 1, JCS Organization—1960-68 folder, box 6, OP-602 File.

27. Ibid., p. 5.

28. Ibid., p. 6.

29. U.S. Naval Institute, *Naval Leadership*, 3d ed. (Annapolis, MD, 1929), pp. 163, 173.

30. Benson Task Force Report, p. F-9. DOD Directive 5010.14 of 4 May 1965 and SECNAVINST 5000.21A of 8 September 1965 directed the services to use the project manager concept.

31. Kennedy, "David Lamar McDonald," p. 347.

32. House, *Communication from the President of the United States Transmitting a Plan for*

the Reorganization of the Department of the Navy, 89th Cong., 2d sess., 1966, H. Doc. 409, p. iv.

33. Lawrence J. Korb, former Assistant Secretary of the Defense in the Reagan administration, noted in his 1979 study of defense policy making: "The first group of service secretaries appointed by McNamara all resigned within a year. To obtain stability, McNamara was eventually forced to place men from his own staff in those posts. McNamara's men really became vice-presidents of DOD rather than heads of the Army, Navy, or Air Force." Korb, *The Fall and Rise of the Pentagon* (Westport, CT, 1979), pp. 86-87.

34. William P. Mack, interview by John T. Mason, Jr., 1979, 2 vols., USNI Oral History, Annapolis, MD, 2: 443.

35. Ltr, McNamara to L. Mendel Rivers, Chairman, House Armed Services Committee, 9 Mar 1966, subj: Reorganization of the Navy, Author's collection. Also in H. Doc. 409, 1966 pp. iii-vi.

36. Ibid., p. 23.

37. Benson Task Force Report, p. F-9.

38. Department of the Navy, *Review of Navy R&D Management, 1946-1973*, prepared by Booz, Allen & Hamilton Inc. (Washington, 1976), p. 87.

39. Benson Task Force Report, p. D-4.

40. Ibid., p. E-3

41. Ibid., pt. 1, sec. 3, Summary, pp. 3-5.

42. Ibid., phase 2, pt. 2, tab G-2, p. 172.

43. Memo, Benson to DCNOs, 25 Nov 1966, subj: Relationships between CNO's Staff and the "Bureaus," OPNAV Reorganization-1966, box 5, OP-602 File.

44. Thomas C. Hone, "Navy Leadership: Rear Admiral William A. Moffett," pp. 83-118.

45. Norman Polmar and Thomas B. Allen, *Rickover* (New York, 1982), p. 208.

46. See Hewlett and Duncan, *Nuclear Navy*; and Polmar and Allen, *Rickover*.

47. Benson Task Force Report, pp. D-5-7.

48. Ibid., p. F-4.

49. Memo, Benson to CNO Advisory Board, 12 Oct 1966, subj: Proposed Structure of CNO's Staff, OPNAV Reorganization-1966 folder, box 5, OP-602 File.

50. F. W. Low, Study of Undersea Warfare, ser 001P003, 22 Apr 1950, pp. 11-12, CNO Studies, Command File.

51. Dillon Board Report, p. 13.

52. OPNAV Notice 5430, ser 130P09B3, 17 Apr 1967, subj: Assistant Chiefs of Naval Operations (ACNO): change in billet titles, OP-09B2 Records.

53. Memo, Director, Long Range Objectives Group to CNO, 2 Aug 1968, subj: OPNAV Staff Organization, OPNAV Staff Organization Concept (1968) folder, box 5, OP-602 File.

54. Briefing, OP-96 for VCNO, pp. 1-2, OPNAV Reorganization (1968) folder, box 5, OP-602 File.

55. Ibid., p. 2.

56. Ibid., p. 3.

57. Ibid., p. 4.

58. Richard A. Stubbing, *The Defense Game* (New York, 1986), p. 285.

59. Memo, OP-090 to CNO, 22 Sep 1969, subj: Growth of Washington Headquarters, 5400, 00-1969 Subject file, OP-09B2 Records.

60. Stubbing, *The Defense Game*, pp. 180. For an example of how defense contractors profited from Total Package Procurement, see the section on the Litton Ingalls Shipbuilding Division, pp. 197-204.

61. Norman Friedman, *U.S. Destroyers: An Illustrated Design History* (Annapolis, MD, 1982), pp. 371, 376-77.

62. Korb, *The Fall and Rise of the Pentagon*, p. 87.

63. Ibid., p. 90.

64. Ibid., p. 91.

65. Lawrence J. Korb, "The Budget Process in the Department of Defense, 1947-77," *Public Administration Review*, 36 (Jul/Aug 1977): 343.

66. Memo, Deputy Secretary of Defense to Secretaries of the Military Departments, 30 May 1969, subj: Establishment of a Defense Systems Acquisition Review Council, 5420 File folder, "Boards and Committees," 00-1969 Subject File, OP-09B2 Records.

67. Mack Oral History, 2: 546-47.

68. Naval Audit Service, "Special Review of the Organization and Mission of the Office of the Chief of Naval Operations and Subordinate Commands in the Washington Area," Report No. S00329, 31 May 1969, p. 8, Review of OPNAV Organization (1969) folder, box 5, OP-602 File.

69. Ibid., p. 9.

70. Ibid.

71. Ibid., p. 13.

72. Ibid., p. 15.

73. Ibid., p. 14.

74. Ibid., p. 11.

75. Ibid.

76. Ibid.

77. Ibid., p. 17.

78. Ibid., p. 18.

79. Ibid., p. 22.

80. Ibid., p. 11.

81. Memo, ACNO, Director of Naval Administration to VCNO, subj: Auditor General's special review of OPNAV: 31 May '69, conducted by Naval Audit Service, OPNAV Audit 1969 folder, OP-09B92 Records.

82. "OPNAV Responses," in ibid.

83. Memo, ACNO, Director of Naval Administration to VCNO, subj: Auditor General's special review of OPNAV, ibid.

6. Zumwalt: Reviving the Service

1. Norman Friedman, "Elmo Russell Zumwalt, Jr.," in *The Chiefs of Naval Operations*, p. 369.

2. *Report to the President and the Secretary of Defense by the Blue Ribbon Defense Panel* (Gilbert W. Fitzhugh Report) (Washington, 1970), Executive Summary, pp. 1, 5, 6, 5400/1 Blue Ribbon Panel folder, Subject files, 00 File.

3. Ltr, Laird to Chet Holifield, Chairman, Military Operations Subcommittee, Committee on Government Operations, House of Representatives, 6 Nov 1970, subj: Military Supply Systems, Creeping Centralization Presentation-1972 folder, box 4, OP-602 File.

4. Memo, OP-09B to CNO via VCNO, 22 Nov 1970, subj: OPNAV Organization, Report of the OPNAV Organizational Review Panel folder, OP-09B2 Records.

5. Elmo R. Zumwalt, Jr., *On Watch* (New York, 1976), p. 285.

6. Memo, OP-03G to OP-090, 23 Sep 1970, subj: Concept of Reorganization, OPNAV Reorganization Concept (1970) folder, box 5, OP-602 File.

7. H. J. Kerr, Jr., interview by Paul Stillwell, 22 Sep and Nov 1982, USNI Oral History, p. 92.

8. Ibid., p. 137.

9. Memo, OP-09B2 to CNO via VCNO, 22 Nov 1970, subj: OPNAV Organization, OP-09B2 Records.

10. Memo, Deputy SECDEF to SECNAV, 14 Sep 1970, subj: Reduction of Headquarters Personnel, OPNAV Organization folder, OP-09B2 Records.

11. Memo, Deputy SECDEF to Secretaries of the Military Departments, 15 Jan 1971, subj: Department of Defense Logistics Systems Policy objectives 1970-1975, Creeping Centralization Presentation-1972 folder, box 4, OP-602 File.

12. "An Overview: DOD logistics management in the 1950's," p. 15, ibid.

13. Deputy Secretary Packard, for example, had argued that the Defense Supply Agency could best manage all the petroleum resources for the services. The Navy opposed this policy on the grounds that it weakened the ability of field commanders to plan operations. The purpose of the Logistics Systems Plan was to guard against such OSD intrusions. Ibid., p. 14.

14. Ibid., p. 15.

15. Friedman, "Elmo Russell Zumwalt, Jr.," p. 374.

16. See Friedman, *U.S. Destroyers* and *U.S. Aircraft Carriers: An Illustrated Design History* (Annapolis, MD, 1983) for discussions on the design philosophies of the FFG-7 and the sea control ship.

17. OPNAV Notice 5430, 5 Mar 1971, subj: Changes to the organization of the Office of the Chief of Naval Operations, OP-09B2 Records.

18. OPNAV Notice 5430, 23 Jan 1971, subj: Office of Tactical Electromagnetic Programs; establishment of, OP-09B2 Records.

19. OPNAV Note 5430, 18 Jun 1971, subj: Disestablishment of OP-97, OP-09B2 Records.

20. OPNAV Notice 5430, 7 Aug 1971, subj: Establishment of the Fiscal Management Division (OP-92) under the Director of Navy Program Planning (OP-090), OP-09B2 Records.

21. Memo, OP-96 to DCNOs, DMSOs, and Chief, NAVMAT, subj: CNO FY-72 Study Program and OSG Officer Utilization, OP-09B2 Records.

22. OPNAV Notice 5430, 1 Mar 1972, subj: Combining MAT-01 with OP-92, OP-09B2 Records.

23. "Fleet Staffs Reorganization Study-1972," Fleet Staffs Reorganization Study-1972 folder, box 6, OP-602 File.

24. OPNAV Notice 5430, 9 Aug 1972, subj: Transferring the functions of the Ship Acquisition and Improvement Division from OP-03 to OP-090, OP-09B2 Records.

25. Memo, CNO to Chief of Naval Personnel, 14 Aug 1972, subj: Officers for Key Washington Assignments, OPNAV/5430 OP-96 1971-79 folder, OP-09B2 Records.

26. OPNAV Notice 5430, 2 Nov 1972, subj: Transferring jurisdiction of the aircraft carrier modernization program from OP-05 to OP-97, the Ship Acquisition and Improvement Division, OP-09B2 Records.

27. "Naval Reserve Command," OP-09E background paper for CNO, 24 Apr 1978, RADM Synhorst's Orig. File folder, OP-09B2 Records.

28. OPNAV Notice 5430, 27 Nov 1972, subj: Redesignating the Director, Antisubmarine Warfare Programs (OP-095) as the Director, Antisubmarine Warfare and Tactical Electromagnetic Programs, OP-09B2 Records.

29. "Establishing Requirements," relating to Secretary of the Navy Instruction 5400.13 of 24 Aug 1971, OPNAV Organization folder, OP-09B2 Records.

30. Memo, T. F. Dedman, Assistant VCNO, Director of Naval Administration to W. H. Bagley, Director, Navy Program Planning, 8 Mar 1972, subj: OPNAV/NAVMAT Organization, Synhorst folder, OP-09B2 Records.

31. Department of the Navy, *Major Organizational Considerations for the Chief of Naval Operations*, vol. 1, *Report*, prepared by Organization Resources Counselors, Inc.

(Washington, 1973), p. V–10.

32. Ibid., p. V–12.

33. Ibid., p. V–14.

34. Ibid., p. V–15.

35. Ibid., p. V–16.

36. Ibid., p. VII–2.

37. [Booz, Allen & Hamilton Inc.], *Review of Navy R&D Management*, 1946–1973.

38. Quoted in Stubbing, *The Defense Game*, p. 327.

39. Memo, CNO to SECNAV, 18 Dec 1973, subj: DOD Headquarters Review, OP–09B2 Records.

40. OPNAV Notice 5430, 3 Jun 1974, subj: Disestablishment of the Office of the Director, Ship/Acquisition and Improvement (OP- 97), OP–09B2 Records.

41. Friedman, "Elmo Russell Zumwalt, Jr.," p. 370.

42. Peter M. Swartz, "The Maritime Strategy Debates: A Guide to the Renaissance of U.S. Naval Strategic Thinking in the 1980s," OPNAV P-60-3-87 (Washington, OP–06, 1987); and Stansfield Turner, "Missions of the U.S. Navy," *Naval War College Review* 26 (Mar/Apr 1974): 2–17.

7. Zumwalt to Lehman

1. Memo, Head, National Policy and Command Organization Branch to Director, Strategy, Plans and Policy Division, 14 Nov 1977, subj: Reorganization, some random thoughts, p. 2, DOD Reorganization folder, box 2, OP–602 File.

2. James K. Oliver, "Congress and the Future of American Seapower: An Analysis of US Navy Budget Requests in the 1970s" (Paper presented at the meetings of the American Political Science Association, 1976), p. 18.

3. Ibid., p. 32.

4. Memo, Assistant SECDEF, Program Analysis and Evaluation, to SECDEF, 4 Feb 1975, subj: Navy shipbuilding, PMS-400 files, Naval Sea Systems Command, DC.

5. See James J. Tritten, *Soviet Naval Forces and Nuclear Warfare* (Boulder, CO, 1986).

6. Memo, OP–09E2 to OP–06, 14 May 1976, subj: OPNAV Strategic/Nuclear Organization, encl: "Review of OPNAV Strategic/Nuclear Organization, p. 1, OP–098 1973–78 folder, OP–09B2 Records.

7. Memo, W. E. Meyer to R. C. Gooding, Chief, Naval Sea Systems Command, 28 Apr 1975, PMS-400 Records, Naval Sea Systems Command, Washington, DC.

8. Thomas C. Hone, "The Program Manager as Entrepreneur: AEGIS and RADM Wayne Meyer," *Defense Analysis* 3 (Fall 1987): 197–212.

9. Victor Basiuk, "Organization and Procedures for Selection of Priorities in Navy R&D and Acquisition," Jun 1979, pp. 10–15, OP–09B2 Records.

10. National Security and International Affairs, OMB, "Review of Naval Material Command Organization," Aug 1976 (revised Sep 1976), Major Observations Section, Analysis of CNM folder, OP–09B2 Records.

11. OPNAV Notice 5430, 21 Jan 1977, subj: Transferring non-RDT&E weapons functions from OP–985 to OP–06, OP–09B2 Records.

12. Memo, VCNO to CNO, 3 Mar 1978, subj: Presidential Reorganization Project, 3 March 1978, Mar-May 78 folder, Synhorst's Original file, Mar-May 78 folder, OP–09B2 Records.

13. See Department of Defense, *Departmental Headquarters Study, A Report to the Secretary of Defense*, DOD Reorganization Study Project (Washington, 1978).

14. Memo, Synhorst to CNO, 25 Dec 1977, subj: Departmental Headquarters Study Project,

Synhorst's Original file, OP-09B2 Records.

15. Memo, SECDEF to Secretaries of the Military Departments, 7 Apr 1979, subj: Establishment of Defense Resources Board, DOD Reorganization folder, box 2, OP-602 File.

16. Memo, OP-09E to VCNO, 6 Sep 1977, subj: Secretariat/OPNAV Relationships, Mar-May 78 folder, Synhorst's Original file, OP-09B2 Records.

17. Donald Stoufer, interview with author, 20 Jul 1987 (hereafter Stoufer Interview). The Office of Program Assessment (OPA) was created in 1962 in response to a Dillon Board recommendation.

18. Comptroller General of the U.S., "Suggested Improvements in Staffing and Organization of Top Management Headquarters in the Dept. of Defense," FPCD-76-35, 20 Apr 1976, OP-09B2 Records.

19. Memo, Head, National Policy and Command Organization Branch, to Director, Strategy, Plans and Policy Division, 14 Nov 1977, subj: Reorganization some random thoughts, p. 1, DOD Reorganization file, box 2, OP-602 File.

20. Ibid.

21. Point Paper, 2 Nov 1977, subj: OPNAV Organization, OP-602, p. 1, OPNAV Organization folder, box 5, OP-602 File.

22. Ibid., p. 2.

23. Ibid.

24. John B. Hattendorf, "The Evolution of the Maritime Strategy: 1977-1987," *Naval War College Review* 51 (Summer 1988): 14.

25. Ibid., pp. 14-15; see also OPNAV Notice 5430, 14 Jan 1980, subj: Establishing OP-00K, OP-09B2 Records.

26. OPNAV Notice 5430, 19 Oct 1978, subj: Eliminating the concept of sea control and power projection sponsorship, OP-09B2 Records.

27. Office of the CNO, "The Maritime Balance Study, The Navy Strategic Planning Experiment," 15 Apr 1979, Executive Summary.

28. Ibid., pp. 11-13.

29. Basiuk, "Organization and Procedures for Selection of Priorities in Navy R&D and Acquisition," p. 8, OP-09B2 Records.

30. Ibid.

31. Ibid.

32. Ibid., p. 10.

33. Ibid., pp. 9-10.

34. Ibid., p. 11.

35. Ibid., pp. 12-13.

36. Ibid., p. 13.

37. Ibid., p. 16.

38. Ibid., p. 18.

39. For a description and critical review of the Maritime Strategy, see "The Maritime Strategy," U.S. Naval Institute *Proceedings* 112 (Jan 1986 Supplement).

40. OPNAV Notice 5340, 15 Jan 1980, subj: Changing OP-095 from the Director, Anti-submarine Warfare Programs to the Director, Naval Warfare, OP-09B2 Records.

8. Resurgence of the Navy Secretariat

1. Memo, Deputy SECDEF to the Secretaries of the Military Departments, 27 Mar 1981, subj: Management of the DOD Planning, Programming and Budgeting System, p. 2, Author's collection.

2. Ibid., pp. 3-4.

3. Ibid., p. 6.

4. Memo, Deputy SECDEF to members of Defense Resources Board, 14 Nov 1984, subj: Enhancement of the CINCs' Role in the PPBS; see also OP-901R Memo, 8 Mar 1985, subj: SPRAA Briefings to Service Chiefs—Potential DRB Issues, Author's collection.

5. John F. Lehman, Jr., *Command of the Seas* (New York, 1988), p. 237.

6. John Fedor, Deputy Chief of Legislative Affairs, interview with author, 1985, Author's collection.

7. Stoufer Interview.

8. Ibid.

9. Ibid.

10. Ibid.

11. Lehman, *Command of the Seas*, p. 265.

12. Two memos, which summarize actions taken after the Boston, VA, meetings of 7 November and 19 December 1986, are in the author's collection. See also Lehman, *Command of the Seas*, p. 240.

13. Memo, CNO to SECNAV, 10 Dec 1982, subj: Restructuring of Systems Analysis Functions, OP-6 folder, OP-09B2 Records.

14. Memo, VCNO to Distribution List, 28 Mar 1983, subj: Restructuring of Systems Analysis Functions, OP-96 1980 folder, OP-09B2 Records.

15. OPNAV Notice 5430, 6 May 1983, subj: Consolidation of OP-OOX and OP-OOK, OP-09B2 Records; Jake Stewart, conversation with author, 22 Dec 1987.

16. Lehman, *Command of the Seas*, pp. 240-41.

17. Ibid., p. 438, note 1.

18. Ibid.

19. Memo, CNO to VCNO, 7 Sep 1984, subj: Navy Headquarters Review, OP-09B2 Records.

20. Lehman, *Command of the Seas*, p. 242.

21. Ibid., p. 244.

22. House Committee on Armed Services, Subcommittee on Investigations, *Reorganization of the Department of Defense: Hearings* [H.A.S.C. No. 99-53], 99th Cong., 2d sess., 1987.

23. Joint House-Senate Conference Committee, *Goldwater-Nichols Department of Defense Reorganization Act of 1986: Conference Report*, 99th Cong., 2d sess., 1986, H. Rept. 99-824, p. 64.

9. Conclusion

1. John L. Byron, *Reorganization of U.S. Armed Forces*, National War College Strategic Study (Washington, 1983), p. 7.

2. David L. McDonald, interview by John T. Mason, Jr., 1976, p. 139, USNI Oral History.

3. See Herbert Kaufman, *The Administrative Behavior of Federal Bureau Chiefs* (Washington, 1981).

4. Peter Drucker, *Concept of the Corporation* (New York, 1946), p. 309.

5. Gene I. Rochlin, Todd R. La Porte, and Karlene H. Roberts, "The Self-Designing High-Reliability Organization: Aircraft Carrier Flight Operations at Sea," *Naval War College Review* 40 (Autumn 1987): 76-90.

6. Craig L. Symonds, "William Veazie Pratt, in *The Chiefs of Naval Operations*, pp. 69-88.

Bibliography

Primary Sources

Archival and Special Collections

The major collections used in the preparation of this study are located in Washington, D.C.: the records held by the Organization and OPNAV Resources Management Division (OP-09B2) in the Pentagon; the files of the Plans, Policy, and Command Organization Branch (OP-602) of the Office of the DCNO for Plans, Policy, and Operations (OP-06) held by the Operational Archives in the Naval Historical Center; the U.S. Naval Institute Oral History Collection and interviews conducted by the author, copies of which are in the Operational Archives; and the Navy Department Library, which holds the major organizational studies cited in the work.

Congressional and Executive Documents

U.S. Congress. House. *Communication from the President of the United States Transmitting a Plan for the Reorganization of the Department of the Navy.* 83rd Cong., 1st sess., 1966. H. Doc. 409.

——. *Reorganization Plan No. 6 of 1953, Relating to the Department of Defense.* 83rd Cong., 1st sess., 1953. H. Doc. 136.

——. Subcommittee of the Committee on Armed Services. *Reorganization of the Department of Defense: Hearings* [H.A.S.C. No. 99-53]. 99th Cong., 2d sess., 1987.

U.S. Congress. Senate. Committee on Department of Defense Organization. *Report of the Rockefeller Committee on Department of Defense Organization.* 83rd Cong., 1st sess., 1953.

——. Committee on Naval Affairs. *Unification of the War and Navy Departments and Postwar Organization for National Security: Report to the Hon. James Forrestal Secretary of the Navy* (Ferdinand Eberstadt Report). 79th Cong., 1st sess., 1945.

U.S. Congress. Joint Committee on the Investigation of the Pearl Harbor Attack. *Investigation of the Pearl Harbor Attack: Hearings.* 39 vols. 79th Cong., 2d sess., 1946.

Bibliography

————. *Investigation of the Pearl Harbor Attack: Report.* 79th Cong., 2d sess., 1946. S. Doc. 244.

U.S. Congress. Joint House-Senate Conference Committee. *Goldwater-Nichols Department of Defense Reorganization Act of 1986: Conference Report.* 99th Cong., 2d sess., 1986. H. Rept. 99–824.

U.S. Statutes. *National Security Act Amendments of 1949.* Public Law 216. Vol. 63, pt. 1, 1949.

Report to the President and the Secretary of Defense by the Blue Ribbon Defense Panel (Gilbert W. Fitzhugh Report). Washington: July 1970.

U.S. Department of the Navy, *United States Navy Regulations, 1920.* Reprint. Washington: Department of the Navy, 1979.

Published and Unpublished Studies

Byron, John L. *Reorganization of U.S. Armed Forces.* National War College Strategic Study. Washington: National Defense University, 1983.

U.S. Department of Defense. *Departmental Headquarters Study, A Report to the Secretary of Defense.* Washington: 1978.

U.S. Department of the Navy. *Major Organizational Considerations for the Chief of Naval Operations.* Vol. 1, *Report.* Prepared by Organization Research Counselors, Inc. Washington: 1973.

————. *Navy Organization Study* (Roy S. Benson Task Force Report). Washington: 1966.

————. "Report of the Board Convened by the Chief of Naval Operations to Study and Report Upon the Adequacy of the Bureau System of Organization" (R. V. Libby Board Report). Serial 05754, 14 March 1956.

————. *Report of the Committee on Organization of the Department of the Navy* (Thomas S. Gates Committee Report). Washington: 1954.

————. *Report of the Committee on Organization of the Department of the Navy* (William B. Franke Board Report). Washington: 1959.

————. *Report of the Committee on Organization of the Department of the Navy.* Washington: 1954.

————. *Review of Management of the Department of the Navy* (Robert S. Dillon Board Report). Washington: 1962.

_____ . *Review of Management of the Department of the Navy*. Study 1, vol. 2, *External Environmental Influences Study*. Prepared under Study Director John V. Smith. Washington: 1962.

_____ . *Review of Management of the Department of the Navy*. Study 2, vol.2, *Planning, Programming, Budgeting, and Appraising Study*. Prepared under Study Director H. A. Renken. Washington: 1962.

_____ . *Review of Navy R&D Management*. Prepared by Booz, Allen & Hamilton Inc. Washington: 1947.

Office of the Chief of Naval Operations. *The Maritime Balance Study: The Navy Strategic Planning Experiment*. Washington: 16 April 1979.

Diaries

Millis, Walter, ed. with the collaboration of E. S. Duffield. *The Forrestal Diaries*. New York: Viking Press, 1951.

Interviews and Oral Histories

Interviews with author.

   Fedor, John. 1985.
   Stewart, Jake. 22 December 1987.
   Stoufer, Donald. 20 July 1987

U.S. Naval Institute Oral History Collection. Annapolis, MD.

   Duncan, Charles K. Interview by John T. Mason, Jr. 3 vols. 1983.
   Kerr, Howard J., Jr. Interview by Paul Stillwell. 1982.
   MacDonald, David L. Interview by John T. Mason, Jr. 1976.
   Mack, William P. Interview by John T. Mason, Jr. 2 vols. 1979.

Secondary Sources

Books

Albion, Robert Greenhalgh, and Robert Howe Connery. *Forrestal and the Navy*. New York: Columbia University Press, 1962.

Albion, Robert Greenhalgh, and Samuel H. P. Read, Jr. *The Navy at Sea and Ashore*. Washington: Department of the Navy, 1947.

Bibliography

Ambrose, Stephen E. *Eisenhower*. Vol. 2, *The President*. New York: Simon and Schuster, 1984.

Paolo E. Coletta, ed. *American Secretaries of the Navy*. Vol. 2. Annapolis: Naval Institute Press, 1980.

Connery, Robert H. *The Navy and the Industrial Mobilization in World War II*. Princeton: Princeton University Press, 1951.

Davis, Vincent. *The Admirals Lobby*. Chapel Hill: University of North Carolina Press, 1967.

———. *Postwar Defense Policy and the U.S. Navy, 1943-1946* Chapel Hill: University of North Carolina Press, 1962.

Drucker, Peter. *Concept of the Corporation*. New York: John Day, 1946.

Friedman, Norman. *The Postwar Naval Revolution*. Annapolis: Naval Institute Press, 1986.

———. *U.S. Aircraft Carriers: An Illustrated Design History*. Annapolis: Naval Institute Press, 1983.

———. *U.S. Destroyers: An Illustrated Design History*. Annapolis: Naval Institute Press, 1982.

———. *U.S. Naval Weapons*. Annapolis: Naval Institute Press, 1984.

Futrell, Robert Frank. *Ideas, Concepts, Doctrine: A History of Basic Thinking in the United States Air Force, 1907-1964*. Maxwell AFB, AL: Aerospace Studies Institute, Air University, 1971.

Hewlett, Richard G., and Francis Duncan. *Nuclear Navy*. Chicago: University of Chicago Press, 1974.

Historical Division, Joint Secretariat, Joint Chiefs of Staff. *Chronology, Functions and Composition of the Joint Chiefs of Staff*. Washington: Joint Chiefs of Staff, 1979.

———. *A Concise History of the Organization of the Joint Chiefs of Staff, 1942-1978*. Washington: Joint Chiefs of Staff, 1980.

Hurley, Alfred F., and Robert C. Ehrhart, eds. *Air Power and Warfare*. Proceedings of the 8th Military History Symposium. U.S. Air Force Academy. Washington: Office of Air Force History and U.S. Air Force Academy, 1979.

Kaufman, Herbert. *The Administrative Behavior of Federal Bureau Chiefs*. Washington: Brookings Institution, 1981.

Korb, Lawrence. *The Fall and Rise of the Pentagon*. Westport, CT: Greenwood Press, 1979.

Lehman, John F., Jr. *Command of the Seas*. New York: Charles Scribner's Sons, 1988.

Love, Robert William, Jr., ed. *The Chiefs of Naval Operations*. Annapolis: Naval Institute Press, 1980.

Naval Air Systems Command. *United States Naval Aviation, 1910-1970*. Washington: Department of the Navy.

Palmer, Michael A. *Origins of the Maritime Strategy: American Naval Strategy in the First Postwar Decade*. Washington: Naval Historical Center, 1988.

Polmar, Norman and Thomas B. Allen. *Rickover*. New York: Simon and Shuster, 1982.

Prange, Gordon, with the collaboration of Donald M. Goldstein and Katherine V. Dillon. *At Dawn We Slept: The Untold Story of Pearl Harbor*. New York: McGraw Hill, 1981.

Rearden, Steven L. *History of the Office of the Secretary of Defense*. Vol. 1, *The Formative Years, 1947-1950*. Washington: Historical Office, Office of the Secretary of Defense, 1984.

Shapack, Arnold R., ed. *Proceedings Naval History Symposium*. U.S. Naval Academy, 27-28 April 1973. Annapolis: U.S. Naval Academy, 1973.

Stubbing, Richard A. *The Defense Game*. New York: Harper & Row, 1986.

Thompson, Wayne, ed. *Air Leadership*. Washington: Office of Air Force History, 1986.

Tritten, James J. *Soviet Naval Forces and Nuclear Warfare*. Boulder, CO: Westview Press, 1986.

U.S. Naval Institute. *Naval Leadership*. 3d ed. Annapolis: 1929.

Zogbaum, Rufus F. *From Sail to Saratoga*. Rome: S. Nilo, n.d.

Zumwalt, Elmo R., Jr. *On Watch*. New York: Quadrangle, 1976.

Articles

Coletta, Paolo E. "Louis Emil Denfeld." In *The Chiefs of Naval Operations*, pp. 193-206. Edited by Robert William Love, Jr. Annapolis: Naval Institute Press, 1980.

Bibliography

Friedman, Norman. "Elmo Russell Zumwalt, Jr." In *The Chiefs of Naval Operations*, pp. 365-79. Edited by Robert William Love, Jr. Annapolis: Naval Institute Press, 1980.

Greenwood, John T. "The Emergence of the Postwar Strategic Air Force, 1945-1953." In *Air Power and Warfare*, Proceedings of the 8th Military History Symposium, U.S. Air Force Academy, 18-20 October 1978, pp. 215-44. Edited by Alfred F. Hurley and Robert C. Ehrhart. Washington: Office of Air Force History and U.S. Air Force Academy, 1979.

Hattendorf, John B. "The Evolution of the Maritime Strategy: 1977-1987." *Naval War College Review* 51 (Summer 1988): 7-28.

Hone, Thomas C. "Navy Air Leadership: Rear Admiral William A. Moffett as Chief of the Bureau of Aeronautics." In *Air Leadership*, pp. 83-118. Edited by Wayne Thompson. Washington: Office of Air Force History, 1986.

————. "The Program Manager as Entrepreneur: AEGIS and RADM Wayne Meyer." *Defense Analysis* 3 (Fall 1987): 197-212.

Kennedy, Floyd D., Jr. "David Lamar McDonald." In *The Chiefs of Naval Operations*, pp. 333-49. Edited by Robert William Love, Jr. Annapolis: Naval Institute Press, 1980.

Korb, Lawrence J. "George Whalen Anderson, Jr." In *The Chiefs of Naval Operations*, pp. 321-30. Edited by Robert William Love, Jr. Annapolis: Naval Institute Press, 1980.

————. "The Budget Process in the Department of Defense, 1947-77: The Strength and Weaknesses of Three Systems." *Public Administration Review* 36 (July-August 1977): 334-46.

Rochlin, Gene I., Todd R. La Porte, and Karlene H. Roberts. "The Self-Designing High-Reliability Organization: Aircraft Carrier Flight Operations at Sea," *Naval War College Review* 40 (Autumn 1987): 76-90.

Rosenberg, David A. "American Postwar Air Doctrine and Organization: The Navy Experience." In *Air Power and Warfare*, Proceedings of the 8th Military History Symposium, U.S. Air Force Academy, 18-20 October 1978, pp. 245-78. Edited by Alfred F. Hurley and Robert C. Ehrhart. Washington: Office of Air Force History and U.S. Air Force Academy, 1979.

————. "Arleigh Albert Burke." In *The Chiefs of Naval Operations*, pp. 263-319. Edited by Robert William Love, Jr. Annapolis: Naval Institute Press, 1980.

Schratz, Paul R. "Robert Bostwick Carney," In *The Chiefs of Naval Operations*, pp. 243-61. Edited by Robert William Love, Jr. Annapolis: Naval Institute Press, 1980.

_____ . "John B. Connally." In *American Secretaries of the Navy*, Vol. 2, pp. 911-23. Edited by Paolo E. Coletta. Annapolis: Naval Institute Press, 1980.

_____ . "Fred Korth." In *American Secretaries of the Navy*, Vol. 2, pp. 925-39. Edited by Paolo E. Coletta. Annapolis: Naval Institute Press, 1980.

Symonds, Craig L. "William Veazie Pratt." In *The Chiefs of Naval Operations*, pp. 69-88. Edited by Robert William Love, Jr. Annapolis: Naval Institute Press, 1980.

Turner, Stansfield. "Missions of the U.S. Navy," *Naval War College Review* 26 (March/April 1974): 2-17.

U.S. Naval Institute. "The Maritime Strategy." *Proceedings* 112 (January 1986 Supplement).

Wadleigh, John R. "Thomas Sovereign Gates, Jr." In *American Secretaries of the Navy*, Vol. 2, pp. 877-93. Edited by Paolo E. Coletta. Annapolis: Naval Institute Press, 1980.

Papers

Mason, Gail. "Organization of the Navy Department: A History from 1947 to 1970." Paper prepared for the Naval History Division, Washington, 2 October 1970.

Oliver, James K. "Congress and the Future of American Seapower: An Analysis of US Navy Budget Requests in the 1970s." Paper presented at the meetings of the American Political Science Association, Washington, 1976.

Index